End the Con

A Plan to Take Back Our America by:
Tom Kawczynski

Table of Contents

An Honest Introduction

The two things you most need to know about me are that I am honest, and I am also stubborn. I don't back down or back away from an uncomfortable truth merely because it is inconvenient or impolitic. And for better or worse, I've never been afraid to make enemies when that is the cost of fighting for what I believe to be right.

In the abstract, these might sound like values that are worth supporting, but I have learned firsthand there is a very high price for speaking truth to power in the age of political correctness. It has already cost me my previous job, my career, my reputation, and a good number of my so-called friends. However, my eyes have also been opened up to the scale and scope of the problems here in these United States in a way few can likely appreciate, and I've taken up these new challenges with vigor.

I've read enough books from political candidates over the years to know they rarely say things of consequence, choosing instead to focus upon painting a happy biography, vague optimistic visions, or ever more grandiose but empty expressions of patriotism. This is not that sort of book. I believe the American people care far more about what a person will do for them than in reading a life account, and that you need to understand some very ugly truths. It brings me little pleasure to share some of my own conclusions, as they are harsh and will likely force policy decisions that will be painful to good people, yet my own conscience obliges me to make the case no one else seems willing to say.

This book will go into detail about policies and institutions, how America has become corrupt in every way, how both parties are part of the problem, and how we have government agencies that manage to escape any accountability for their wrong-doing. More fundamentally, we are trapped in a never-ending death match between two competing systems, and in this struggle, we've lost sight that the purpose of a just government needs to be to serve the interests of the American people. We have a Democrat Party which cares more for foreigners than citizens because they want the votes from a future they are deliberately creating, and want to pander to their minority base which has hijacked their party wholesale, whether they realize it or not. No better are the Republicans who up until recently would have sold out their own mothers for a nickel and considered it good free market ideology, facilitating what has been a wholesale replacement of the traditional American people and sending our jobs elsewhere.

I know I'm not going to make any friends amongst any of the elites by sharing these common-sense truths, and suspect before this campaign is done, I might very well be the most hated person in America to some. I can live with that, so long as I also know what I am sharing with the people, and this movement I am trying to catalyze to reclaim truth and to begin fixing our beloved country, present you with the information you need moving forward.

I am beyond politically correct. I am sometimes offensive. I make comments about all types of people, and assert not just our right, but the fundamental necessity that we learn to critically analyze the actions of those with whom we share this society. To that end, I have made comments critical of Whites, Blacks, Latinos, Asians, Jews, Native Americans, men, women, Christians, Atheists, Muslims, gays, straights, and it goes on and on. Such honesty has landed me on more than one "hate list" for being a supposed racist, bigot, xenophobe, anti-Semite, etc. Unlike others, I don't let such branding silence me and don't apologize for describing what I genuinely observe. I've done this before, will do it again, and trust people have enough discretion to discern humor from genuine prejudice.

I believe in reason. Reason requires we look at how people act, both as individual actors, and in terms of group tendencies. When people do things we perceive to be harmful, we must be able to comment upon them and offer correction if we are to protect our own self-interest. Once, such logic was easily understood, but we live in a bizarre media environment where certain groups are held to be above rebuke, and to even comment upon things they actually do is deemed an infringement against social norms. I reject this convention and will comment upon whomever I please, encouraging others to do the same so we can have actual dialogue instead of being constrained by fear.

For such honesty, people who speak out are slurred with epithets and labeled hatemongers. To be clear, I hate no man or woman for the circumstances of their birth and have publicly stated that all people should feel pride in their origins and capacities. This statement would seem uncontroversial at first, but as a proud White man who speaks up for his own people, who make up over sixty percent of America and whose ancestors primarily built this country, I recognize these ideas formed the foundation of our past even as the media reviles any who speak in favor of the majority.

If you're reading this book, it probably hasn't escaped your attention that the ongoing anti-White jihad from the Left is constant and unremitting. They literally would have you believe that loving Whites is worse than being a serial killer with how they cover this in the news, but we all know that is absurd. They would tell you that the fact we appreciate our own folk automatically entails that we must hate everyone not like us. Yet they never apply that standard to the identity movements of any other race in America, all of which they proudly and loudly blast to the public. Such an absurd double standard is so obvious that even its purveyors have to notice it. So, what's really going on?

I believe the powers that be fear White identity and nationalism because these forces, coupled together, can form the basis of a defense against a socialist takeover of America that has long been in the planning. Because when one looks critically at who is voting for what policies and candidates, a very clear pattern emerges that is reshaping America, and no one is willing to talk about it. The pattern is as America continues picking up more population which comes from the Third World, which is to say Latin America, Africa, and poorer parts of Asia, those people overwhelmingly are voting to make this country more like the places from which they originally emigrated. And this applies even more strongly to their children and grandchildren when they reach voting age. My earlier books cover this in much more detail, but the summary is that every other group besides Whites are increasingly and reliably voting as a bloc, all driven by the Left to vote to take from the majority to fund their coalition of the ascendant into control of the future.

We are told this transformation is inevitable. It is not. It has been the result of years of manipulation by our government and our politicians against the interests of the traditional American electorate. There was nothing inevitable about allowing over a million people per year to enter our country, nor in the chain migration or amnesty policies enacted by both Right and Left. This happened beneath all of our noses because the White population had been a majority for so long, and we assumed our values were universal, so we didn't realize the system was being gamed. Now, we have to stop and consider how to move forward.

I believe fully in self-determination, and I think we as Americans have to decide right now, while there is still time to reverse these trends, if we want to continue down the path to becoming a second Mexico or even Venezuela. Your

Congress and previous Presidents didn't give you a choice. They merely promised this would never happen and proceeded to vote for the precise opposite as they began with the Hart-Celler Act of 1965 which has added tens of millions of people who come from very different cultures.

Immigration is a big piece of the puzzle, but it only happens because we have a corrupt media that lies constantly and propagandizes the American people against their interests. The corrupt media attacks decent Americans while serving as mouthpiece for not just the Left, but also a perverse globalist vision, and has many allies all through education which teach our children to hate America. No one ever talks about this, but it's time we start fighting back to teach our children to love this country and their forebears. Furthermore, we must cease funding these people who only seek to demoralize and degrade us. I have some ideas on how we can restore balance to what is taught, because I don't want to monopolize the conversation – I want to see all sides be fairly heard.

It is worth noting the attack on identity has become equally blatant against defenders of traditional morality, with none receiving the blows more harshly than Christians. Despite the clear reality that it is only in nations which were of primarily Christian origin that strangers and non-believers have been welcomed to participate with equal status, the lie propagated is that people who practice grace and mercy are now considered hatemongers and beacons of injustice. The people who cynically tell these lies know they are false, but do so anyway because they seek to strip us of our morality, and of a means by which we can both judge what is being done to our homeland, and from any calling to a higher authority than to the state which is being set up to be nearly a God unto itself in the powers and authorities to which it lays claim. We have seen what happens when the State assumes such sanction, especially when people overwhelm us who vote to enact such policy.

As oblivious as people inside the Beltway seem to this, we see a shroud of censorship creeping across America from the far right moving ever closer to the center. People are kicked off platforms for violating ever-shifting "community standards," which is another way of saying not adhering to politically correct dogma. I want to see our government stand in support of free speech standards across the Internet, stop the ridiculous idea that voices should be silenced for having unpopular opinions, and allow you, the people to decide what you want to hear. Freedom of speech is meaningless without the freedom to listen and access to multiple streams of information. Americans should be worried at the growing links between big technology companies like Google and the governments of countries where they are silencing dissent, both abroad and here at home.

I start with these topics because unless we can speak honestly and without fear of censorship or recrimination, we cannot begin to address the basic policy issues impacting America today. I talk about immigration also here because the choice we're forced to make is whether we are going to try to pay for everyone to have what they want, or if we will finally become more selective about who we let in here. We need to fully understand the immense social costs of both legal and illegal immigration, and that the current path is depriving our own people and our children of opportunities and resources they desperately need.

I believe we could have low taxes, improved health care, a high level of security and freedom, and a cleaner safer nation, but we need to stop bringing in people from outside, and we need to have the courage to send the people who do not belong here back to their homelands. To do this, we need to face our fears about being called dirty names and being attacked by the left, and this is why I never back down from pride in my identity – even as I encourage others to always assert the same. I temper this with morality and the knowledge and good grace that still yet endures in these latter days where our civilization is under such challenge.

I also think, once we become more united, we can tackle some of the big issues we need to address. We need to stop thinking we should police the world and getting into useless wars in the sandbox. We need to roll back the power high finance and the media wield over us, which is why I support localizing media and ending the Federal Reserve system. We need to look at seriously reforming our entire intelligence apparatus as it has become a rogue state within DC. None of these tasks will be easy, but if the people are to be sovereign once more, all of these tasks are necessary.

Seeing the urgent necessity of this agenda, and seeing no one else acting upon these issues, I've decided to put myself forward as a man willing to speak to these topics and to start an honest conversation with the American people. I have many flaws, do not have all the answers, and pray to the Lord that I am equal to what I am trying to do here. Our country deserves so much better than what we have, and we're running out of time, because the demographic reality is such that soon democratic solutions will likely only go in a negative direction.

I don't have a lot of resources, and I don't have a great name, but I have the truth on my side and faith in the decency and integrity of the American people. We have an unmatched capacity to come together and achieve what must be done to secure our republic and remove the corruption and the rot within our body politic. It is with my hope in you, or rather a shared faith in us, that I start this, as what I hope will become a viral, people-driven campaign, against corruption and waste and to restore America closer to the vision of our founders.

This book will be about me and my ideas, and how they will impact and help you and your family. I'm going to start by describing how I look at problems so you get a clear framework that makes far more sense than either a state or market driven system, and what the plan to fix Washington will be. It only works with a lot of help, including not just votes, but candidates and leadership at every level. I'm not going to pretend this will be easy, but haven't you noticed politicians who say as much are usually robbing your back pocket when they make such promises?

That's why the central theme of this campaign is "End the Con" Because the people can do far better than our political class has done, and though we're going to talk about some hard topics that are painful, I think we can come out the other side with better understanding and the ability to reunite to take back this country. We are going to enumerate what is being done to us, and begin this vital conversation about how to reverse this corruption and return power to the people as is just.

Nationalist, Populist, Traditionalist, Realist

Given the many challenges which exist in reforming Washington, I think it vital we have a clear mental framework about how we will seek to address these issues. We've seen many well-intended efforts from all sides fail to change very much – not just because of the financial and institutional support for this corruption, but also because of the ease by which any effort to change things is quickly divided into new contours of the same partisan game. Once DC converts a new argument back into an "us versus them" approach along the old Republican versus Democrat line, people begin voting once more for their preferred animal and the zoo resumes. That isn't going to be good enough, and we're seeing right now with the present administration the limitations of what can happen once a reform minded candidacy gets shifted into purely partisan status. Literally, the entire Democrat edifice has shifted policy positions on foreign involvement, border security, and economics just to ensure the balance endures, keeping the creatures of the Swamp comfortable and well-fed.

Having established the necessity for a different mental approach, I personally use four criteria to consider issues, and these are what I will push for us to use as American people in how we seek to transform our government to something more useful. The first key concept we need to unfailingly embrace is **nationalism**. Nationalism simply suggests the responsibility of the American government is to always consider first, foremost, and singly the interests of the American people in its operations. It is not the job of our government to serve foreign interests, global needs, hidden oligarchs, special interests or some external system.

Let's start with the latter because while people might presume our government inherently would serve our interests, I encourage you to think of how both the State and the politicians who refuse to fix it actually think and behave. "By their fruits ye shall know them," it is written. Judge by their deeds and results rather than their words. If, over an extended time their results trend a certain way and they have not altered course, you can be assured those results are what they actually desire.

Overwhelmingly, politicians come into the public sphere with a certain ideological mix wherein they believe either market-based outcomes must prevail, or the state should exert dominance to favor certain results.

Those in the former camp tend to think of everything in financial terms, and their mindset – which dominated the Republican Party for many years – came to believe that selling jobs overseas was a good thing because it would sustain their ideal of perpetual economic growth by always seeking new markets and labor sources. Such thinking hollowed out the Midwest, destroyed our industrial base, and moved our wealth onto paper. Many working Americans were simply left behind while the new orthodoxy moved away from productive wealth to simply paper and ledgers. The economy moved from one where wealth resulted from innovation and production to an economy where wealth is concentrated via interest, fees and ever-more-opaque paper shuffling. It was a shameful betrayal of a whole class of our people, which we are only beginning to rectify and realize now, but it happened as a logical extension of putting systems thinking: Unfettered faith in the market, above people.

The Democrats, for all their feigned empathy, are no better. Their desire to force socially just outcomes has led them toward a dark path toward totalitarian rule. The free speech hippies of yore have given way to censors who support beat mobs to silence those who speak against any and all who offend the politically correct orthodoxy that sees society as a hierarchy of victims. The victim classes, and new ones are created daily it seems, are to wait in line and be judged by them, the leaders, to determine who will receive what share of the loot they seize from those who produce but have been deemed to be historically advantaged. Their Utopian dream of realizing economic equality through redistribution alone has them considering tax rates that would make Stalin proud with no limitations to how far they will go. People look at what they say and laugh thinking they're just pandering, but I assure you, they are very sincere. The progressives are on a mission to create the heaven here on Earth they do not believe exists elsewhere, and they are taking over that party just as they now control so much of the education system.

But their obsession with equality, which I'll cover in more depth slightly later, is just another example of systems thinking, and why at the heart of their belief, they've stopped caring if the government helps Americans or foreigners. Because just like the Republicans who see people now as dollar signs, the Democrats just see people as mouths to feed, and anyone hungry is worth looking out for in their way of viewing the world. In neither case does their thinking ask the most vital question: Who are our people and how can we support them?

This is where I start with nationalism as a third way. We live in a world with limited resources. While no person of good conscience wants to see anyone else suffer, our government lacks the capacity to most fully satisfy the needs of its own people when those leading do not focus their efforts strictly toward the benefit of those already here who are legal citizens of this country. While we can and should work with other nations for mutual benefit, America has occupied a position such that we have upheld an international system by agreeing to disadvantage ourselves for many years, and that price has been paid by the American people, specifically the poor and middle classes who have dealt with increased crime, increased cost, lower quality jobs, and a reduction in the standard of living that is only slightly beginning to abate now.

I give Trump credit for putting us on this different path, and will seek to aggressively accelerate and expand this within the Republican Party. Years ago, our government and media stopped discussing our standard of living, because it has been on a continual downward slope for decades. Instead, they have harped on stock market averages, which merely represent potential profits for a very small class of people, as opposed to the well-being of Americans as a whole. Trump has seen this and, albeit only slightly, his rhetoric and some of his policies have at least started to address the problem.

Although nationalism transcends partisan affiliation, specifically because it elects to choose from either state or market-based solutions according to the needs and desires of the people, rather than the dictates of an orthodoxy, the truth is the Democrats are so wedded to universalist egalitarianism they cannot be reformed. We see the proof of this in how they work more vigorously to defend the prerogatives of caravans invading this country as opposed to the working poor who still vote for them because they perceive no better option. Conversely, within the Republican Party, we've seen how the market thinking is giving way in many quarters to the understanding we must put Americans first, before making a dollar, and to understand culture cannot perpetually be subordinated to economic efficiency.

In recognition of this, I propose the Republican Party re-brand itself as the National Republican Party, a sign of commitment to all our citizens that we will honor two important ideas. First, that Americans will always be considered the sole concern of our leadership moving forward, instead of how neoconservatism hijacked this party into foreign adventurism and how neoliberalism sent our money and jobs abroad. We reject class, but accept citizenship as an active and meaningful term, a two-way street where we begin demanding more of our people, but in turn, offer more in response. Second, that we honor the Republican brand by recognizing, as did our Founders, that the form of government specified by the Constitution is that of a Republic with deliberately enumerated powers, rather than a democracy. This republic was specifically designed to protect the essential liberties of our people, bestowed by God and cherished by tradition.

Such nationalist thinking will present a clear counterpoint to the universalist concept that currently pervades both parties. Instead of believing there is a perfect system, we only seek to realize a better people, and we do not want to force conformity to some preordained conclusion. It is honest, it is sustainable, and it allows us to begin rebuilding unity. Instead of fighting incessantly with each other about who is right, maybe we could work together against a world that isn't that fond of us anymore.

A **populist** approach to policy is the only way a nationalist can govern, where we deliberately look for policies that the people desire and that would also work to their benefit. Contrast this thinking with how our system currently works, where we have elitist leaders who sit in echo chambers on certain coastal corridors, and enact policies most people do not like, and are contrary to their well-being. The wars overseas are the perfect example where a majority of citizens, whether they vote Democrat or Republican, do not want to see our patriotic soldiers used to play geopolitics or endangered for corporate profit. Yet the elected officials of both parties are literally threatening sanctions to counter our Commander in Chief's proposal to bring them home to the safety of their families and for the protection of our homeland. For too long, elites have treated our men and women as their playthings, and those days must end now.

I am sure like many other Americans, you're sick of all these grand causes we're told America must fight. I'm sick of wars in the Middle East where we all know nothing will change from the mess it has been the last few thousand years. I'm sick of hearing how climate change means everyone has to ride a scooter and that we need to slaughter every cow because their farts are destroying the atmosphere. I'm sick of all this media promoted crap, and of how media giants have perverted their protected position that was created to inform the populace into lying and propagandizing us relentlessly against our own interests. For too long, these people have been trying to transform America into something antithetical to its founding principles and hostile to its heritage population, instead of celebrating and elevating our people, and I intend to call them on it because we can do far more than people think.

We live in an age where new media is rising, and you can trust me to make sure freedom of speech conveys through to freedom of information. I will fight censorship, of points that either agree or disagree with mine, because as a core value, I think we need to promote dissent as healthy and get past this idea that someone being offended means society must go silent. There are many people who are going to be offended during this campaign and most deserve every one of the insults they've been able to dodge for far too long. Because I reject the idea there are protected classes who exist beyond rebuke, and this whole farce of "hate speech" is an elitist trick designed to make us forget reason, and silence legitimate opposition.

It may very well become obvious as this campaign advances that many in Washington serve unpopular interests because of financial incentive and foreign connections. It seems obvious to state, but we should not allow our government to be lobbied by foreign money, yet this is a daily occurrence in the District of Columbia, and as a nationalist and populist, I pledge to remove those people from being able to buy America as their servant.

Instead, we're going to listen pragmatically to the problems in this country and use our resources to our benefit. Functionally, this means a lot less involvement abroad as those funds are needed for the good of our own people. It means our defense will be defensive instead of seeking to intervene constantly throughout the world. But it also means we're going to take a broader scope of where government should be involved than has traditionally been the case on the Right.

I talk about this in far more detail in some of my earlier writing, but I think the people who care about principles and limited government have made a strategic error in just letting the universalists and elites use government as their tool while taking a hands-off approach themselves. In practice, this means leftists and globalists advance their own agenda through government anytime they are in power, but conservatives unilaterally disarm so that whenever they hold power, they only serve as a slight pause in the achievements of their opposition. Even though I agree the letter of the law often suggests such restraint, by exercising restraint when the leftists and globalists will not, we've functionally made the decision to abdicate control over our society through such choices, and it is costing us our culture and our society. As a nationalist, I accept there are times the Federal government might be the best option to address issues, and that pragmatism of knowing an imperfect solution we might offer is better than the alternative that will be thrust upon us is needed to govern. Because if the people demand something, and we say no, then all that will happen is they will seek leadership elsewhere.

Such responsiveness is new and messy, but it shifts us onto ground where when we talk policy, we'll be talking about what matters to people. We will cover better health care, clean environments, less crime, and more affordable and more pro-American education. As nationalists, one thing which really helps us is that all the money we will save by not taking care of foreign countries or foreign invaders, can be used toward our people, their enrichment, and building a stronger America.

Sadly, our elites don't care about that, because they're above being American. They're globalists who feel more comfortable in their various enclaves protected by their wealth and above the law. Not in this country, not any more. Here, we serve Americans.

To honor our past, restore our future, and minimize the suffering involved in these difficult challenges, we should be proud **traditionalists**. Our country has much worth defending, but unfortunately our civil society, honored faith, the nuclear family, and even the concept of America itself have been battered and abused for years by elites who want us to so hate ourselves that we give power that is rightly ours over to them willingly without complaint.

Instead, our people should recognize the root of our problems was not a lack of kindness or consideration, but if anything, an excess of generosity that was misplaced within our society as well as invested in people who saw their future as not being bound with our own. It was our innate sense of fairness, and willingness to question ourselves in seeking a better future that has led to such doubt and eventual despair that we've now stopped defending our culture, our nation, and our civilization. How can one have a sane country when the majority hate themselves and when they try to disown their own past? All we end up with is an empty state waiting to be occupied, which is what the radical egalitarians want, and precisely what we must oppose.

The conservative instinct to mistrust government is entirely justified, and a more forceful resistance against the encroachment of the state into so many areas of life would have been timely indeed. But with past efforts having failed to restrain the war on our culture, we must be stronger than we once were and proudly claim our traditions as our own., Instead of being content with anemic attempts to conserve what has already been lost, we must be proactive in rebuilding a new future guided by our traditions, while adapting those traditions to our present scenario by recognizing the timeless principles of liberty, authority, our Christian ethics, and our limited state, and seeing how they fit the challenges we face today. We must be as sure in our search for excellence, which Western Civilization once celebrated, as those who want to impose equality upon us are in their efforts to unmake us if we wish to compete.

The final point as we consider how to fix America is we must be **realists.** When someone suggests a policy to me, I want to know if it will work. I find that far too often Americans have created solutions to problems that sound comprehensive, but functionally don't address the core issues. Often, this happens because it is impolitic to state the actual roots of a problem, and a commitment I make to you is to be blunt and sincere in seeking the causes of our problems so they can be addressed effectively at their roots.

That's one reason you'll hear me talk about immigration so often in a racial context. I would prefer very much if I could simply say new people coming into America are just like previous entrants and vote as distinctive individuals. Some do, but the numbers suggest a very different story which is at the heart of my policy thinking: People behave both as individuals and as part of larger group entities. We're both, and so it's not right to say group identity is everything or that it is nothing. It's something, and we need to understand it, instead of pretending it is evil to acknowledge this reality.

I took a year to think about this and to write about these questions in exhaustive and painful depth, and I've come to see a two-step solution as just. Respect the individuals but acknowledge the trend. For those people who demonstrate they are realists who love America and liberty, we should honor them as active and beneficial citizens who have much to offer. But we should also see there is an ever-growing bloc of people who are just here to take what they can get, cynically for their own, across all races and groups, and admit they are of little value to our efforts going forward as they are.

How we limit their ability to destroy our future is a question we must ask, because the reality is, we are now in a zero-sum game of identity politics begun by the Left and over which they have most likely lost control. As people of good character and resolve, we need to contain this threat, hopefully through better education, opportunity, and migration policy, but ultimately through whatever means required lest we become a socialist hellhole. Such language is harsh and stark, but when you look at what the globalist elitist visionaries dream up in contrast to this sane vision, I fear I am being too restrained in describing the magnitude of the threat.

But as realists, we must admit the major fights of our time will be here at home and realize we have to choose between whether we will continue the foundation of our forefathers both in spirit and in form, or if we will instead accede to the intended transformation of America into something else. I can only tell you that, having studied history my entire life, there is no one more committed to preventing the emergence of something terrible in this nation than yours truly, but the time to act is limited and we must begin acting now if we hope to accomplish this without tragedy.

This challenge is open to all Americans of good conscience, across all races, who understand how delicate our situation has become, that liberty only endures in a society of trust, and who want to move past the problems of identity politics to realize a new cultural norm, shared overwhelmingly between us all, as a means to reconstruct this nation and restore the values which have served us so well. The challenge is immense, but it is worth noting that multiculturalism, in reality, is killing us and so we must fight that battle directly or nothing else proposed can hope to save any of us.

Choose Excellence Over Equality

I believe Western Civilization has one really terrible disease we need to overcome, and it is an obsession with equality. Perhaps my historical perspective colors my views a little bit here, but I believe some time after we emerged from the Middle Ages and as the Renaissance and Enlightenment created a new hope in Europe and America that man could take mastery over this world, the idea that we, as people alone, could create a perfect world based upon our own knowledge began to percolate. The age of nationalism, based upon understanding that different people are discrete groups of culture, language, tradition, and kinship, gave way to the age of ideology and the maniacal demand that the right belief could convert everyone to some singular unity.

Where the old system had borders and the mature recognition that different groups were successful specifically because they held different beliefs suitable to themselves and had tangible borders between them to allow separate spaces for independent development, the new thinking was that justice and progress demanded everyone be subject to the same system. It's easiest for our minds to think of Europe this way, but frankly, the same thing happened in its own way here in America as our individual states have been separated from the autonomy they once enjoyed within the Union to being increasingly just lines on a map and subject to Federal jurisdiction. But this path has not been without consequence, as social tensions have arisen specifically because people are no longer permitted to choose alternative paths but are pushed ever more toward one equal path we're told we all must walk.

What is equality really? Everyone uses the word, although sometimes in ways that are contrary to its actual meaning, but the simplest and most honest definition is sameness. To be equal to another is to be indistinguishable from them. As much as the advocates for forced diversity would grate at this explanation, the inevitable outcome of their plans is to uphold conformity, reduce distinction, and make people into less. Excellence is an affront to equality, which is why words like "discriminating," "supreme," and even "better" are attacked today as being hateful.

If you think about it, why wouldn't people want to be better? Why wouldn't we seek the best of ourselves and celebrate others who find that for themselves? Why shouldn't we seek to discern which values and concepts are best, and speak against those which are less optimal? Reason demands such for the world to function, as basic causality works this way, and you would use such diagnostics for medicine, machinery, or any other function. But in society, we are told we cannot make such judgments.

Statements such as the foregoing are hurtful to some people, and because we are afflicted with an obsession with equality, we are not allowed to make anyone feel like they might be less than anyone else. We are not allowed to say that crazy is crazy anymore, and should you dare to challenge this orthodoxy, you will learn firsthand just how much power is behind this dark dogma.

Since we cannot make judgments without giving offense, we've literally morphed into a strange country where feelings are used as a substitute for reality, and where if someone imagines themselves a thing, then socially they are granted that status. If a boy imagines himself a girl, then according to today's definitions, he can be. Some find this liberating and rewarding as it attempts to unshackle the human spirit from nature itself.

Others, like myself, find this logic insane. I told you that I'm a realist and as part of that I believe nature has rules, reason allows us to understand them, and we live best when we are in the world of reality and not fantasy. I also believe a boy is a boy and a girl is a girl, and at some core level, it stuns me that something as basic as core biological identity has been thrown into disarray, but this demonstrates just how far the social engineering has spread that has deliberately confused our society away from asking the basic question we've long since seemed to forget.

In the West, we've forgotten how to make ourselves better. We have retreated into our respective fantasies, all claiming victory by saying each of us wins by merely being ourselves. But the consequence of such a universal victory/non-victory in fantasy-land is that our society existing in the real world is falling apart. The roads crumble, the people become callous, and our aspirations have become entirely internalized. Since we can't argue, we don't. We just retreat away from ugly arguments over values, against the tiring rhetoric of what is best or what is good and claim it doesn't matter.

Although without precedent in scope and scale, especially in America, there is historical context for this in Rome and elsewhere. Late empires give way to comfort and decadence, depravity taking the way of civic virtue, and we see civilizations collapse. We see that here in the West where every country of our civilization is being overrun with our elites celebrating the demise. Old barbarous cultures, which at least have the consistency of their belief, are given free rein to use force to live, breed, and change the world back to a simpler form specifically because no one cares to fight for the old corrupt civilization.

This happens because no one who claims to fight for equality *truly* fights for equality. In truth, when people say "equality" in politics, they usually mean envy of wanting to have things those with more possess than they do. In practice, this leads to systems of redistribution whereby those who don't have take from those who do, and those who used to work, stop doing so because it makes no sense to try so hard just to lose what they should have earned. It's easier to describe in economics than culture, but the same problem is happening culturally as well.

We used to have a culture that dreamed of national goals. We aspired to go to the stars or conquer new frontiers of the mind and science. But now we only ask how we can feed more mouths and pay more damages. I'm not against a little humility and humanism, and not without a mind for charity, but we stopped believing we could do anything good anymore, and that's what happens when people obsess over equality – we exist only in envy, fear, and loathing, and stop celebrating or seeking our own potential.

How do we break this trap? We need to start celebrating excellence, stop apologizing for what we do well, and be unafraid to make judgments. It's better to make some wrong decisions than to be unwilling to make assessments at all, and I certainly live by those terms. I hold strong beliefs based upon things I think to be right, many of which I know will offend, but all of which I believe to be true.

As just a sampling: I think children have a better opportunity to succeed with two parent families, with a mother and a father, and that the state should work to encourage that behavior. I think marriage exists between a man and a woman, for the purposes of having children. I believe while it is not the purpose of the state to persecute anyone for their departure from social norms, I also believe it is harmful to our future to idealize sub-optimal solutions and pretend they are great, to make people feel good when in the demonstrable world in which we must reside, they are less likely to succeed.

To say two parents are better than one gets you called a hate monger. To say gays living together isn't really marriage gets you labeled a bigot. But do you know what it also does? It creates the space to discuss what is best for the children who have no choice about being thrust into such arrangements of self-serving adults, because we are only here a short time, and we should always be asking how we can leave a better tomorrow for our children. And we can't ask that question if we are so immersed in our own feelings and entitlement that we cannot admit that allowing everyone to be a snowflake comes at a price to others, including children, who have no choice but to pay the tab.

Now, I know people who oppose my thinking will read this and deliberately misconstrue everything above to say I'm going after people who think differently than I do. I will certainly contest them, but you have the right (or at least should have the right) in this country to associate or dissociate with whomever you choose. I wouldn't threaten that. But I am going to spend a lot of time talking about what is healthy, and I hope we can begin doing real research to see what leads to the best outcomes.

For too long, it seems to me we've been forbidden to ask certain questions because some people in positions of authority assert certain answers must be true. We have to say all races are equal, all genders are equal, all everything is equal, and they're clearly not. We're not the same, and all differences between groups are not superficial. None of this means that any of us are less deserving of respect and essential human dignity. In truth, it is only through honestly admitting our differences that we can get along, realize our own fullest potential, and maybe begin to see what we can do with America from where we are today.

I know what I'm asking is hard and will require many awful conversations because equality, with no demands other than less of people, is very easy. I can only demonstrate my willingness to pay the price as my wife and myself have been pilloried by the media and by insane activists who have threatened us, for saying such basic things as "White people don't actually suck," and "Christians are loving people." In this age of envy and resentment, taking pride in one's self is seen as a sin by certain quarters, and this campaign will be attacked for daring to promote excellence and bringing back the idea we should seek the best in ourselves and our country.

I think we need to seek out a new Manifest Destiny, and I pick that term specifically knowing the controversy it will cause, because we need to shake ourselves out of this foolish reverie. We need to seek our better selves, and my challenge to all Americans is to become the best version of yourself and admit what you do well and what you do poorly. Let us admit our strengths and weaknesses, address them, and find a common best path as a new single culture to unite us. We will always allow dissent and diversion, but please recognize that the opposite of diversity is the very unity we need for our nation to endure, compete, and grow. We need to have faith in ourselves and in each other, and we can't do that if we hate each other or ourselves.

I don't resent the success of anyone. I celebrate that. There are times it is hard, because I'm a traditionalist, and like many people, I don't understand fully the world being created around us. I try to listen, to read, and to consider, but the speed at which technology and society move is too rapid, and I think we all just retreat. But instead, why don't we ask what we are doing, slow down just enough to get more of our citizens on board, and ask what we must do to make our country something truly exceptional? What can we do together as nationalists working for our own interests?

For too long, I think we've just been adapting to a world changing around us instead of asking the important questions of the sort of world we want to create with the tools technology provides. The unfavorable outcomes we see all around us are what systems thinking in a world governed by money, ideology, or statism will get you. But in a world of people, where we are different and distinctive, we can ask these questions, and maybe create something special. I want to start those conversations, and despite the reality that I can be crusty and difficult, I remain an optimist who wants to seek answers to these questions out with hope and positivity.

This campaign will ask those questions and keep an open door to every citizen, including those who only want to dispute all that I am sharing here. We can always argue who is right and wrong, and what is different, because each time we have the courage to do that, we're fighting back against the malaise of equality where we don't care enough anymore to even try to offer an opinion. It's that indifference that has allowed our subversion for so long, and as contentious as it will necessarily be, we'll have to fight through our differences one way or another to gain sufficient consensus to act if we ever hope to regain control of our own future from those who now cynically guide our state.

Importantly, this also means anyone joining us will be the best people we can have, because they will be the ones who care enough to actually try and fight. I want to connect this back to nationalism, explaining this is the very reason elites hate the concept: because it has the power to unite people in common cause for their collective benefit, seeing that there are many opportunities where we can all benefit, and when we look upon what is happening in our country from that mindset, the corruption and guilty parties become all too clear. They fear that so they stoke us against one another in perpetuity, but I'm here to tell you there are ways conflict can be resolved so we don't fight one another, so we can focus our ire upon those who perpetually set us against each other.

This campaign will be very vocal in identifying those people, even though we will be attacked mercilessly for such honesty. But before it's all done, you're going to be glad I'm as stubborn as I am about these things, because we're going after root causes, not just the disposable henchmen when I start eyeing the swamp for reduction. It is time we make the con men famous and reveal all their dirty tricks, and whether you agree or disagree with my particular suggestions for solutions, we can all work together to assault the hypocrites, charlatans, and swindlers.

The Feckless Republicans

As introduction to this chapter, I've devised a simple three step plan for how we must act to retake our country. The first step is to push aside the sorry corporate excuse for a Republican Party that currently exists and replace it with leadership committed to the national interest and the survival and betterment of our people. The second step is to contain the threat of the radical egalitarians and begin contesting their mastery of the cultural space which we'll talk about in the next chapter. Finally, we must find a way to come to power, and to bridge the divides which currently make America ungovernable. To accomplish that we'll need to listen both to our Founders and to the common sense that nationalism applies, and which has disappeared in this age of ideological warfare.

As people who care about reason, values, virtue, and the traditions of our beloved country, we must start by getting our own house in order. If you ever want a hint about how Republicans feel about their party, ask them how they self-identify. Many will say conservative, whereas others will say libertarian, and a new crop of nationalists have been added to that mix, but what you will rarely hear is people talk about how they are proud Republicans. There's a very good reason for that, because for many years the most fervent supporters of the platform beliefs of this party have been disappointed again and again.

The Republican Party has, unfortunately, become the do-nothing party. I can think of no better example than their many failures during the first two years of the Trump Administration. Despite having a majority in both houses of Congress, and having passed measures to end Obamacare, also known as the Affordable Care Act, multiple times when in the minority, they could not muster the votes to repeal an act their base hated. They did manage to fund Planned Parenthood twice, however, which is an insult to every pro-Life advocate in the party. There was never even a serious push to fund the wall or border security, but instead there were merely increases in the military budgets, more money for foreign adventurism, and a tax cut that overwhelmingly benefited corporations who pressure for endless foreign labor. In other words, nothing changed with Trump getting in there in how our Congress behaved, and even as I write this, I continue to see Republicans undercutting their own President to make a strong border impossible. I'm not surprised.

Many decades ago, the Republicans made a strategic mistake from which they have still not recovered. When the cultural wars of the 1960's were tearing America apart, they decided to take the position that they would be the party to not use government to change society, believing that free individuals and civil society should be left to the people. Such thinking is eminently understandable, but in addition to failing to use government to remake society as the Left has done with glee, they did not use government or private benefit to sustain or preserve the alternatives to government intervention such as the family, the churches, and the various private charities. Instead, they sat back and claimed to be above the fray while the Left began their long march through media, education, entertainment, and culture, remaking this country ever more into their image. As the Left became stronger in their control of the publicly accepted values, they hammered ever harder, and the Right retreated into nostalgia, intellectualism, and the habit of political flight from cities and states alike.

There were warriors who sought to arise to this cultural challenge like Pat Buchanan and the proud paleoconservatives, but they were sidelined by an establishment more concerned with power, money, and influence than stopping the moral decay in America. People who spoke about the culture we were losing were pushed aside, and then labeled by the Left as first regressive, then racists and all the other slurs with which we are now instantly labeled by virtue of being merely right of a "center" defined by the Left alone. The Republicans could have come together in defense of these men, as the base wanted and as good conscience demands, but they chose the easier path of trying to reduce everything, including people, to economics so they would never have to be called offensive. They succeeded in ensuring their own irrelevance, and this is why we now see the Republicans on the verge of being a permanent minority party, because the changing demographics of America the free market people created only lead in the opposite direction.

It was the failure of Reagan, and absent a sea change, it's also becoming the failure of Trump, to think that economics alone and new wealth will somehow preserve the culture and values of limited government, personal liberty, and responsibility. Money can be spent, but rebuilding culture and families is a generational struggle.

I know the GOP likes to celebrate two term Presidents as heroes, but when you let in huge groups of people through either legal or illegal immigration, amnesty or merit, and they consistently vote no less than two-thirds for the opposition, you simply cannot afford victories like that. Why that happens will get a whole chapter of its own later, but the executive summary is that immigration is why California is now a one-party state, Arizona will be gone next, and Texas will be Democrat by 2030 or so. Then it is game over in electoral math and a Republican will never win a national election again. Those estimates are based on official numbers, and officials have a motive to misrepresent such data, so this eventuality may come even sooner than expected.

It's a beautiful lie the Republicans like to tell: That they will somehow convert the people coming here to become just like their natural constituency, and the new Americans will choose opportunity over direct subsidy. A few people do, and to them, I offer all the credit and congratulations in the world, but conservatives should have been skeptical enough about human nature to recognize people will tend to take the path of least resistance given the choice, and the Democrats will always be willing to offer more for less than we could even imagine. Given their generosity with the wealth of America, and the equally ugly truth they basically own the entire culture due to our principled retreat, we cannot even articulate a counter-alternative without being marginalized and shut-down. I live on the far right and can tell you that our best ideas aren't even allowed to be heard without a label being affixed and the censorship and virtue signaling slapped on, with the sorry excuses for Republicans missing no opportunity to punch right to please the media.

That's the Republican leadership in Washington. They signal to the benefit of the Left constantly, meet the obligations of the donors from the Chamber of Commerce and other lobbies to keep the money and cheap labor flowing, and in exchange get a pat on the head from the media as the good and acceptable opposition. So long as they are not too effective, they exist to present the illusion of choice, and are allowed to negotiate compromises always to the benefit of the Left, but where they can say they stood on principle and fought.

Even more sadly, millions of Americans keep voting for these guys as a protest vote against the insanity we see from the Left. We fight to protect our values, to celebrate our heritage, to preserve our liberties, to save the unborn, and we get comforting rhetoric in return. These last few years, we've even gotten a few judges, for which I am grateful and place considerable hope, but when it comes to Congress, we get nothing but excuses. Paul Ryan and Mitch McConnell were a joke, and their successors will be jokes as well because Republicans will vote for these leaders simply because they're not Democrats.

It's not good enough. I know people aren't prepared to just hand over the reins to the crazies to make a larger point, but the only other alternative is what I am proposing here: That we take this party back. For years, patriotic Americans have been seeking a party to represent them, ranging from the flirtation with the Reform Party to the anti-Fed anti-War Ron Paul Revolution to the Tea Party which reminded us our Constitution created a republic and not a democracy where everything is for sale. Now, we add nationalism to the mix as we all want to restore American greatness and stop the sellout of our jobs, our future, and as I will argue, our historic identity. All of these impulses represent different pieces of what I would argue is the same puzzle, but I think the time has come now to unite the pieces in one populist platform and blow aside the corrupt incumbents and their cynical donors with a fresh new wave.

We need a Republican Party that can fight, that believes in this nation, that has an optimistic and assertive vision and is not afraid to wield power to build a better tomorrow. The battle for smaller government was lost, but the struggle for smarter government need not be. So if we can articulate better ways to use government to protect both the liberties of our people and meet their needs, there will be massive popular support and a renewal of our nation that has been waiting decades to start. New generations are not saddled by guilt and fear of what the other side will call us, but instead are ready to fight by whatever means necessary to make America good and great.

What does this look like? I offer my formulation as nationalist, populist, traditionalist, and realist to replace the old outlook of market driven, minimalist, amoral, and dogmatic. We are not abandoning the market, the idea that people should choose their own success, or faith in our heritage, but we can't just sit back and let the Left use government like a scalpel to pick us apart. We can't let them just fund their nonprofits, use their professors, and lie on media to gaslight and demoralize us. We have to call out every lie and become the party of truth, especially when it is painful.

I have a very clear vision of what America should be, with the family as our foundation, respect for our traditional faith, Christianity, love of our heritage in western civilization's achievements through reason and mastery over nature, and in the recognition that European ancestry is worth celebrating collectively and individually. For years, they've beat on Christians as bigots, Whites as racists, traditionalists as obsolete, and marriage as oppression. No more; we need to begin fighting for our values because our future depends upon that, and we cannot sit back and let them demoralize us any further under the false pretense that that they are only lifting up others.

The reality is that the Left is enabling a wholesale change of what it means to be American, who Americans are, and what we must believe. In .the face of this onslaught, we haven't had a party willing to fight them and call out all their crazy ideas. The American people were never given the chance to vote on their lunacy or to fight against their proscriptions, and I believe we should and we must while we still have the numbers to potentially change course. Our current Republicans won't do this because they, including the President himself, believe more immigration is a good thing because they're all obsessed with money and not seeing that bringing people from everywhere into a country which no longer knows who it is will destroy us all.

I am not opposed to economic nationalism, but without a culture to unite us, it will be disproportionately concentrated in the hands of friends of the Federal Reserve, and whatever trickles down will inevitably by stolen by Democrats for their constituencies when the electorate inevitably shifts back the other way as it must. All that money made will then just be used for the social programming we see them promote in ideas like the Green New Deal, which would set America back a hundred years in energy production, transportation, and make us an international laughing stock. But what scares me most is we don't offer an alternative.

As part of reclaiming our manifest destiny, I argue for the American restoration, whereby we can keep our economic gains by rebuilding a single culture based upon our traditional morality, with respect for all and a strengthening of our liberties and Bill of Rights. We can use government to ensure freedom of speech and freedom of arms – and against tyranny endure – and we can begin breaking up these monopolies of culture and technology if they threaten our chance to present this healthier alternative. We can elevate the family, personal responsibility, and stop pretending we can be all things to all people. Using reason, we can be honest about nature, and begin enforcing standards again and bring sanity back to America. I'm here to lead that fight, and I'm willing to take as many arrow pricks as required because I know our good and just people will support and follow this needed message.

I would fight for the National Republican Party and if need be, I am willing to die for it. It will not have escaped the attention of more astute readers that my previous best-selling book was *The Coming Civil War*. The stakes are potentially that high, but as someone who loves our people and peace as well, I'm jumping in here to provide a third way that is neither the conflict that may very potentially come with another decade of inaction or potentially even worse, the submission into a sorry country much like Venezuela that will befall us should we lack the courage and organization to act. I won't pretend that I am always right, but if you want a fighter who isn't going to make excuses and who will listen, I believe I have both the courage and clarity of vision needed to act if others choose to follow.

We live in a revolutionary time. We don't know yet what that will mean, but we will be heard, and America needs better than "good enough" from the Republicans. The good news is all that is standing between us having a strong nationalist party that offers real alternatives to this new generation of progressives is to tell the donors to take their money elsewhere because America is no longer for sale. Now, we fight for our people, for our liberties, and against all this corruption.

The Unhinged Democrats

The Democrat Party isn't what it used to be. While they always had Marxist tendencies, the core of the party was once people from the working class who sought to improve the economic welfare of working Americans. One could disagree with them about the size and scope of government, but their loyalty was to the American people who were born here, went to school here, and lived here. They cared about security, and you could work on policy compromises with them based upon the scale and scope of social programs.

When and how that changed specifically is an interesting discussion, but between the social activism that began in the 1960's, and the cosmopolitan universalism they adopted after the Cold War nominally ended, what is undeniable is the modern Democrat is a progressive of a very different stripe. Their leadership now consists of zealots who are no longer so concerned with the economic well-being of the American people, but instead seek to remake society by declaring war on reality itself to realize greater social justice-based outcomes and to disconnect cause from outcome.

Progressivism is a cult. Even though they might not express it explicitly, their core belief is that a heaven of "equality" can be created here on Earth, and they will stop at nothing to realize that Utopian future. There is no tax too high, no restraint too harsh, and no policy too extreme for them to adopt. A mistake people commonly make when listening to the radical Left is to assume the proposals they put in the public space are exaggerated and they do not take them seriously. Listen to me: Take them very seriously because these are people who are on a mission who believe they are making a better world by destroying all which came before that does not conform to their expectations.

I've sometimes thought they've gone to such an extreme because they have been unopposed for so long by the Right which turtled and retreated into itself, so they just kept pushing further along. When it comes to remaking society, the Left has historically enjoyed the advantage of knowing how to work the dialectic, which is to say they present you two choices, expecting a third option to emerge that is a compromise between the two previous items. They use this technique to present individually reasonable ideas but which create an ever-advancing trajectory toward their ultimate end goal: Total actualized equality.

So, what started out as reasonable impulses to protect civil rights and encourage free speech against the constraints and oversights of the past has now morphed into a rigid politically correct superstructure which has all the joy of a detention room as it seeks to punish people who offend the new orthodoxy which states a person can be whatever they choose so long as they don't have any concern for what any other chooses. Such nihilism is devastating to society, but repackaged as tolerance and diversity, it has become the celebrated hallmark of Democrats and the Left to accept anyone and anything, ignoring the accumulating contradictions that we pay for in our society in increased crime, disunity, and national discord.

Equality assumes that no value is greater than any other. Such relativism is how you can have a party that celebrates Islam, a religion which actually does sanction female genital mutilation and throwing homosexuals off roofs, while including the majority of feminist and gay activists under the same tent. It would seem such bedfellows could not easily co-exist, yet so long as they have a common enemy to keep them focused which is how traditional Americans and our values are presented, they manage to hold dissent at bay.

In addition, you can see the members of the seemingly contradictory coalition as keeping their end of a bargain with leftist government. That is, as long as government gives them what they want, they will fight against traditional America rather than against each other. As long as the gravy train is flowing, this coalition will remain intact unless a particular aspect of it is placed in immediate danger, such as a Muslim member of Congress advancing a bill specifying a death penalty for women who cheat on their husbands.

Anti-Americanism is a natural feature of this new Left because to celebrate what has come before would suggest the past was more just than the future, a forbidden concept in their dogma. This is why from an ideological stance they're more comfortable defending the plight of the illegal invaders they deceptively label "undocumented persons" than their own fellow countrymen in rural Appalachia, because they measure everything in terms of a hierarchy of victimization.

The rhetoric which they present to the general public is that equality will uplift people to a new common center. The reality which they admit amongst themselves is the only way equality can be realized between unlike groups and people is to seek out the lowest common denominators, which requires them to bring people down from success and excellence – which is why they hate the word supremacy so much because it suggests one can rise above – and to essentially force people to under-perform. That's why they love social programs people cannot escape and why they relentlessly try to destroy anyone who imagines there could be a better future, because they are choosing individual or family success above the group. One can see how they are becoming totalitarian.

It would seem that people would abandon this sick belief once they observed its many failures, both domestically and throughout human history, but the vision and ideal that we could all be happy and well taken care of is so alluring many cannot escape its clutches. What helps further are years of indoctrination in schools and in the media to teach that this is how things must be, with generous helpings of false guilt placed upon many of the more successful tiers of society, and the extreme social consequence for heresy.

The other part that is driving this new Left is identity politics. Starting with LBJ, the Democrats made a series of decisions to weaponize race and to use envy to create permanent voting blocs against the Right by promising financial support from the majority to the minority. The consequences of these decisions are now becoming apparent as the Civil Rights successes of that era are now giving way to a new age of fighting over race because the Left chose this battle.

They spent generations telling every minority how evil the majority was, have told them they have every right to own this country and our stuff, and instead of restraining themselves, supported a policy of bringing so many foreign people into America who fit the non-White profile for radicalization that they have now lost their party to these sorts of politics. What was likely rank opportunism has given way to dangerous radicalism.

It is a difficult thing for people to hear, but we cannot escape this challenge now because the Democrats cannot go back to being a party driven by economics. The demographics of their party, to compete at a national level given what they've culturally instructed their minority base and the sympathetic White intellectuals, require them to push further still in transferring wealth and power to the disaffected, both in terms of ideology and identity. After years of Republicans refusing to speak against this for fear of being called racist, decades of submission to this way of thinking from society as a whole has set up a situation where the "coalition of the ascendant" expects to be handed America, and they will likely fight back if that doesn't happen.

I wonder if the Democrat Party leadership knows this. As I watch the Muslim members of the delegation espouse open anti-Semitism and feel no guilt or shame as the older heads of the party try to constrain them, this is but the leading edge of a progressive jihad which is coming to remake America. The Green New Deal will certainly see wealth redistribution prominently featured, and for those who want to resist, the Left has shown time and again throughout history their utter lack of restraint in their willingness to use government to force compliance. When you hear them talking about socialism, you best understand they mean communism by any other name, and having grown up in a country of wealth and fantasy as America has strangely become, so many blindly support these aspirations without understanding their damning consequence.

The problem is no one exists to stop them. As described previously, the weak Republican Party hasn't shown the spine to organize the American center against this plan. The cultural leaders of our society have been endorsing these programs, which is why we really need to begin questioning why our corporate media is so eager to see such destruction wrought on an America that has served them so well. We need to wonder why the professors who do so well are so angry, and we can talk about these many reasons as we will during this campaign in ways that will confuse, confound, and likely offend. It's not an easy puzzle to resolve why

America is so dead set upon undoing itself, but I believe the obsession with equality is the mental trap at the heart of this sick puzzle.

As this campaign evolves, one need only watch the Democrat primary to see what they believe in their own words. You will see relentless pandering to every issue group they have and every fringe identity. They will stumble over one another as quickly as they can manage to demonstrate who can virtue signal best, and reality will go entirely out the window with the promises they will make to their voters. More importantly, after Trump's term in office, they will promise action and punishment against those who took power from them because as true believers, these people have already demonstrated they will show no restraint in how they will use government to remake society.

If they come to power, they will either make America into something that is the precise opposite of what our Founders intended, or they will push the other side so hard that conflict will become inevitable. I don't know precisely what form that will take, but this see-saw battle must come to an end if we are to survive as a nation, and we can't be a country of liberty and opportunity if half our people are determined to wholesale change who we are to make us all equal, whether we want it or not.

So, even though I come as an emissary from the Right, I can only say for the sane people who support the Left because they care for the people and perceive, somewhat rightly, that the other side has been indifferent to their concerns. There is a place where we can converse based on reason and an honest assessment of the nature of things. Nationalism is not heartless to the struggles of the poor and working class, instead targeting the elites who actually lead this Democrat programming which is setting us against one another.

Multiculturalism is disunity. So is diversity. We can have differences, but without the search for essential unity, we cannot long survive the challenges ahead, so I throw this challenge out to the reasonable folk on the Left of all creeds and colors: Stop believing in the fantasy that we can all be the same, and let's see if we can start to work this out on a more sustainable basis.

As for the new leadership rising in the progressive ranks, I know these true believers will have to be confronted with a clear moral vision that rebukes their plans to undo all that exists in America. We know they will push for more social programming, so look for them to further sexualize children through the transsexual agenda. It's a neat trick the Left has perfected to get people so immersed in the particulars that they miss the larger problems they create. Namely, that they destroy all connections that are natural and healthy in society.

My first book *Someone Has to Say It* went into exhaustive depth on how this works but consider how feminism has set women against men to the detriment of all. Now, we don't have nearly so many families that raise and love children, but instead we see the state inserted as intermediary, allowing the ideologues in the progressive camp to reach our children even earlier to teach them the gospel of secular equality. But, for all their supposed progress, are we any happier? Ask the cat lady sipping her thirtieth Chardonnay if a pay check and a studio apartment in a metropolis that won't notice if she dies ... was worth the cost of being able to bring life into the future and have a loving partner beside her?

I use that one example, but there are plenty more that demonstrate how our entire society has been deliberately divided so many times into new factions and fights, all so we would surrender more power to the state. This is not just an unhappy accident, but the deliberate planning of cultural Marxists who want yet another shot at what they failed to achieve in the old Soviet Union, and we are honestly walking right into this trap. We walk out of it when we acknowledge we can all be more, can be different, and choose to strive toward personal and societal excellence.

We don't have to always agree upon what is right to realize what is wrong, and there are few things less American than trying to force conformity so that everyone talks just like everyone else. Culture has to be more organic than that, and while I am certainly a fan of seeking a new unity, the way the Left is going after this can only end in tragedy. As such they must be opposed vocally and stopped by whatever means required.

Lastly, just as I have rebranded the Republicans as the National Republicans, we should not allow the Democrats to masquerade their intent any longer and you will hear me refer to them as the Socialist Democrats from here on in. Their goal is to game elections by spiking their numbers to remake society into their vision where people don't matter, but only their support of this terrible and beautiful system to which they have fallen subject does.

The Third Way: Authority and Liberty

It doesn't take a genius to realize this system isn't working. So many people are not being served at all by this government, the elected officials answer more to donors than voters, the bureaucracies do whatever they like with near total impunity, and we've ended up with a schizophrenic tendency to shift the country entirely in one direction and then in the other leading to policies which make little sense with gridlock to follow and national decay as the result. This might be why as much as half of the electorate or sometimes even more chooses not to participate in national elections, especially on the off-year cycle. Something must be done to get us on a better track.

Nationalism is important here because it resets the conversation in a way that is not ideological. Though some could argue that nationalism is an ideology, it is instead a *hierarchy of values* for making decisions in which the people of a nation, and the structures that give birth to that nation, such as families, are prioritized as the standard of value against which decisions are measured. Nationalism stands against the corruption that permeates both the establishment Left and the establishment Right, as both prioritize many things above the well-being of Americans.

Given what sorts of measures are being advocated today, and that we literally have members of both existing parties demonstrating their greater concern for the affairs of non-

Americans, whether they be through policies like sanctuary cities on the Left or frankly how foreign policy has used the US military like a mercenary force for other countries on the Right, both are shameful examples of the leadership not putting Americans first. We should reconnect to a clear and unwavering standard that all people in government be primarily concerned with our citizens.

Citizenship is an important concept which needs to mean more than where one was born. Citizenship is only meaningful when the rights it conveys are balanced by the responsibilities it requires. For example, a young man who has not registered for Selective Service is unable to obtain a student loan. Unfortunately, this is one of the very few areas where the balance is maintained, where the more common practice has become to think only of satisfying obligations to the citizens without any larger social responsibility.

Whenever rights are conveyed to a person without corresponding responsibilities required, that balance is nevertheless satisfied by requiring others who have no say in the matter to sacrifice. Over time, small gaps become chasms and we witness the ludicrous situations prevalent today in which hard-working responsible citizens are forced to pay excessive taxes to subsidize the rights of irresponsible people. Or you see traditional Americans being unable to effectively exercise their right to speak freely so that children can be forcibly indoctrinated by government schools in a gay or transsexual agenda. How long can an ever shrinking few carry the weight to maintain a whole nation?

Citizenship, properly understood, conveys a responsibility on behalf of the person to invest in society beyond what they can simply take from government. We used to understand in America that our people, each one striving to achieve their greatest potential, made our country great, and now we've forgotten that. You can see the evidence of this past throughout the small towns and cities of America. If you look carefully, you'll see parks, monuments, hospitals and music halls that were built by people who volunteered to give more to society than they took away. That is one of the great keys to maintaining and building upon civilization: citizens who shoulder the responsibility to make contributions that will last even beyond their own lives.

This has been a key aspect of America since its founding, and the attitude is reflected in the preamble of the Constitution in the phrase "for ourselves and our posterity."

But this is also seen in the outpouring of human excellence in products and innovations that make life better than it would otherwise be. It isn't money alone that makes this possible– it's the hard work behind those products and innovations. It isn't government itself, because bureaucracies seldom seek excellence. While government can sometimes help by clearing a path or providing funding, it would be foolish to rely strictly on such help because it makes our people dependent upon the restrictions and welfare of others when better options exist.

To restore culture, we need to rebuild citizenship as a concept, and this is where I demand much more from anyone else in this race. I speak often of the import of using our reason to command mastery over nature and to build, on the basis of realism and traditionalism, a better future. But that means we need to start holding one another to account, and we can't simply go into tomorrow with a culture where we assert we will tolerate anything and everything uncritically. Liberty demands we give people a wide berth for self-determination, but even such latitude must have its limits and we need to see the restoration of a national culture of virtue and excellence.

This will be a conversation rather than a dictate, and it will have softer edges rather than hard contours. We need to talk about values, honestly, and the problems we face in society instead of just blaming one another. I believe there are certain values that are not compatible with a future worth experiencing, and I think there are also certain time proven beliefs like respect for marriage, our traditional Christian values, and hard work that deserve defending. I also oppose certain ideas, like the wholesale importation of people from the Islamic world or the ongoing sexualization of our children, and want people to know that it is healthy for society as a whole to make judgments that certain things should not be publicly supported.

To protect liberty, we need new authority in terms of moral leadership to discuss that which is healthy and that which is not. This conversation has long been suppressed because of the fear of over half of America to speak their mind lest they face social ostracism or other penalty. The radicalized Left and their allies in the media have destroyed far too many lives just for speaking sanity and common sense, and a big part of what this campaign is about is to make it so they can never do this again. We will face them, we will reason over them, and we will not let them intimidate us anymore.

An America based on excellence instead of equality will be unafraid to speak about what will give us the best society today and tomorrow. It can be an optimistic place with hope and driven by achievement, and we can hopefully learn from the many disputes we face today. Maybe, we can even move toward the essential unity we lost when we divided into our own little clans and factions, because if we don't do so soon, I've said as a matter of public record that I think a much larger fight is coming. You simply cannot have two diametrically opposed visions of truth co-exist atop one another indefinitely in the same political space without there being a massive consequence.

As we determine these values, we need to hold our people to account in how they follow these precepts and how we work together. For so long, the evolving American model has been a cynical effort where new people are just being imported into this country by the millions to change the voting patterns to help the Left, while claiming that wholesale population replacement to achieve socialist outcomes is "democracy." I believe our immigration failures are the biggest voting fraud scheme in history, and we need to start seriously asking if the people brought here belong. Because I don't accept the idea that we are obliged to give our country away, and I think the obligation our government owes is to our citizens, our principles, and to the framework our founders created. Democracy like that isn't very democratic at all, because it represents a predetermined outcome that was selected for you, often in direct contravention of the liberties we are all guaranteed.

Instead, we are going to recall that America was founded as a republic where powers were deliberately limited and decentralized. While as a nationalist, there are times where, for the unity of the nation, I believe we need Federal level solutions, I also believe in the republican ideal of returning powers to local governments and individuals whenever possible. Most importantly, when it comes to economic power, this matters most as it gives you the economic freedom to act in your lives.

Where I do think differently is in how national leadership needs to speak to cultural issues, and instead of simply surrendering the floor, we're going to look at what people are doing in America and whether their actions are building up our country, making it more united, or if they are just subverting the desire for a better future. There's a lot of hatred for this country that passes itself as legitimate criticism, and I suspect a closer inspection will see many foreign actors and questionable entities behind these acts. Sunshine has ever been the best solution for corruption and bringing these ideas into the open will only help.

As we discover what isn't working, what we will provide is firm leadership designed to remove the corrupting agents and restore basic competence to our government. We will seek to rein in agencies which serve their own narrow interests, and we will be very willing to remove those who fail this mandate, and reform those which can be saved. In this, I think of the entire federal intelligence and law enforcement apparatus who have clearly demonstrated an unhealthy symbiotic relationship with the national media, a frankly illicit willingness to interfere in elections, and a gross failure of their duties. The FBI has done a particularly miserable job these last few years and have no one to blame but themselves for their own politicization.

My general inclination is to not trust systems, and part of what a nationalist renewal will require is examining each agency and area of government to see if they fulfilled their duty, as well as the needs of the American people. Where Trump wanted to drain the swamp, I will show no restraint in going further in setting those old and rotting edifices on fire so we can clear space for new growth. Certain institutional cultures are just too far gone to be preserved, and with entities like the unaccountable Federal Reserve, we're definitely going to be looking to return power to the people.

I know such honesty will make me many enemies, but we cannot fix America without addressing the deep-rooted causes of why this government doesn't represent our people. We have to deal with corrupting money, foreign intervention, deceitful bureaucrats, and the cynicism of the parties themselves. We need to remove each, and in the policy section of this book, we'll go into some detail about ideas I have to begin the restoration.

But I suspect that should this process really get started, we might discover there won't be much of government left to rebuild. I'm mentally okay with that, because I know nearly 90% of Americans mistrust Congress, and huge majorities feel the same way about every other major agency except the military. This is a revolutionary process we're talking about to reset America from a corrupt system to a healthy nation, and our government will never be the same. But it should be much better, and the key to all of this is your willingness to hold all sides to account.

The final result will be something different than we have today in ways that are difficult to predict, but I suspect legal reforms and financial reforms will play a huge role. We certainly can't continue to have campaigns and a lobbying system so awash in money that our government is essentially put out for the highest bidder. I wonder just how many of our elected representatives are simply mouthpieces for other entities, and it's something we need to discover with the help of patriots around this country.

I think we would end up with a smaller and leaner government that will be less involved in people's daily lives, but that has a firmer hand in certain specific areas to encourage national unity and achievement. My vision of manifest destiny is where we conquer ourselves and push ever onward toward a better vision of a freer and fairer country but with high standards, high ambitions, and self-determination. This new America, having given the blood of generations to the world for its security, has earned the right to invest in itself without apology, and I don't see us playing policeman any longer. It's a small world, and we'll need to work with others in peace, amity, and mutual respect.

That I speak speculatively here is an honest admission that I don't know how deep the rot goes and what pieces will remain once we begin fighting corruption. I do know, however, that those invested in the status quo won't like this. The media will tell every lie known to mankind, which is what they do best. Remember, it can't be called a free entity when everyone working there is getting paid. Who do they really serve? Because it's certainly not the people.

I suspect just as we see now, there will be a flurry of red tape designed to deny and distract. One thing we can do is begin declassifying all sorts of information about what our government has been doing, and if I should succeed, we're going to learn about what happened to Kennedy, and every other sordid act that has happened since but has been suppressed under an overly broad assertion of "national security." Because I've seen the biggest threat to American liberty, and for many years, it has been our very own government.

So, you could go with one of the usual candidates, who will promise a variation on a familiar theme that has been historically proven to fail, or you can look at me, because I am offering something different. I'm offering strong leadership to solve the problem of why America is no longer working as it should. You could vote for more of the ping pong game, or you can take this moment before identity politics consumes all into a maelstrom from which we will likely not escape and figure out who set us on these disastrous paths. Then, having found the guilty parties, we can have a stronger America emerge which honors our own revolutionary past, is proud of its history and all its constituent peoples, and where corruption will receive the harsh punishment warranted for deceiving the people. It is a different path than anyone else is promising and will require a strong national movement and a lot of patience and forbearance from us all, but I'm willing to try and at least speak out for a great country that has a new lease on life awaiting, if we only have the courage and vision.

We can restore our nation and we can heal the divide, but we need to take down all those who screwed us first, and then be clear that we can no longer be everything to everyone, but instead select our new national beliefs and move forward in unity. That is the struggle before us, and this campaign is a beginning toward that important work. While it may very possibly take multiple cycles to realize, we will either succeed here as we pass the quarter millennium since our founding, or we will see America as it was imagined lost to the sands of time as history marches on in another direction. The choice is ours.

Allow me also to share that while nationalism is presented as a scary word, designed to intimidate those who don't look a certain way, you need not be frightened if you don't fit the majority. Help in building a culture of which we can all share and be proud, and this will be a home for you and yours far better than any country from which any of us emerged, whatever your specific origin. I will not pretend this will be easy, but I am utterly certain the price of pretending unity doesn't matter will cost us all, with the strong suspicion those who are in the minority now being set up to take the brunt of any future cost, which is something no man should willingly accept for his own.

The First 21ˢᵗ Century Campaign

This is a different sort of campaign. I've been involved with a campaign or two over the years and have seen how they are usually top-down affairs with rigid message control and trying to bring resources into a war chest to pump out commercials and pay consultants telling you how the opponents are pieces of crap and how the candidate is the best person ever. We're not doing that. I'm not the best person ever – I'm a real pain sometimes – but I'm honest. And as for my opponents, you can judge them for yourselves.

Instead, this is going to be a campaign which is highly decentralized, driven by personal connections and social media, and where there isn't going to be just one message. It starts with a series of questions, the first being the theme of this campaign: *"End the Con."*

The statement is designed to bring people forward who have long been pushed into silence and bring forth the truth as you see it and share the common sense observations about a system that has long been broken. I know millions of Americans have watched what has been happening in our nation with dread and disgust and have been quietly fuming about our degradation. I want you to come forward, let people know what isn't working, and reach out to your friends and your family. Your support would be nice, but frankly, it isn't about me so much as stimulating a national moment to bring up all the dirt we've swept under the rug so we can honestly address why we're at the verge of fighting one another.

We are blessed to live in a time where it has never been cheaper or easier to share conversation, and using the Internet and real life in equal measure, we're going to start conversations. I want people talking, and I want uncomfortable ideas to come into the open. We're no longer going to embrace the shadow of political correctness behind which this cult of equality operates, and they cynically use to force decent folk to restrain their honest thoughts. I'll take the blows from the blowhards who are on the air so that we can talk once more and offer a beginning to important national conversations.

I encourage people to share what they hear in their own distribution channels, making this campaign their own, and to help us identify all the sources of corruption both within government and without so we can look at what they've been doing. Be funny, be creative, and don't be afraid to offend. Anything has to be better than this current discourse of lies and apologies that we watch farcically played out each day.

Even though I admittedly come from the edgier portion of right, because we've been under assault for so long, we've learned how to operate our ideas like an insurgency, and I want to share the benefits with you. If you have to act anonymously, that's fine. I understand we're not in an

America yet where free speech is permitted without consequence, and I know the censors will be looking to terrorize once more behind community standards and false pomposity. What I am saying is I want to give voice to the idea that the majority doesn't need to be afraid to speak out any more for the values we always had, but which we're now told are wrong, even as every fiber in my being informs me they are right.

We will coordinate our attacks by a very simple principle: Tell the truth when you see it and call out lies and hypocrisy everywhere they arise. It isn't hard to see a thousand different examples of how our leaders each day promote one policy for one group but call it evil for another. Frankly, the treatment of Whites as a group not allowed to love ourselves is what brought me off the bench, because I got sick of seeing every other race celebrated and told that we, who make up 60% of America, are terrible beings for having built this country and allowing others to come live amongst us. I simply can't take such nauseating drivel anymore, and I'm going to call these people out.

We all have our personal battles, and yours will be different than mine. But we can all participate in calling out the lies and double standards, and in this, I hope you will help. This is how we fix our culture, by being willing to show what is obviously broken and false, and to attack the many little lies which service the big one that holds us hostage. We assume equality, but we are not equal. To be free, everyone needs to stop trying to be like everyone else, and to stop even pretending this would be a good thing.

I'm going to take my message to anyone who will listen, although I'll tell you right now I intend to deal with the national media as little as possible. They have long been the enemy of the people, actively propagandizing us to hate one another for their own cynical benefit, and as biased partisans who have the social ethics of prostitutes with less friendly service to boot. I know they will lie about me and lie about us because we threaten their power, and they fear populism and nationalism because it would displace them as elites who arrogantly tell you what to believe and think, and might even see them held to account for the many deceptions they've perpetrated.

Instead, I'm coming directly to you, the people, and I'm going to work through independent and social media to put my message out as intended. I know I say and think some controversial things, and we can talk about all those ideas. I usually think I'm right, but I might be proven wrong, and I want everyone to know I'm approaching this as openly as my conscience allows so that we can come together. It's no secret that I have been a critic of how hard it will be to hold America together given how different some of our people are, but it deserves my best effort, and I'm trying hard here to find the narrow path through which the most people can walk alongside us. Compromise will be necessary from time to time, and if the dialogue is genuine, I accept this as the price of maintaining peace which is well worth paying.

Obviously, we're going to need help to make the ballot and to raise enough money to meet the legal requirements for how this campaign will work. If you can give, I appreciate the help. I'm not looking to build a war chest of people who write $2,500 checks so much as to build a stable base of donors who can kick up $20 to $100 per month for the chance to fix this country. I know that's a lot to ask, but this will never be a campaign driven by the wealthy and their interests. I'm not against them, and won't refuse any generosity, but it's a populist campaign.

I also know, sadly, that in America today, one can be punished for their political contributions. I've seen this happen again and again with hate groups like the SPLC and ADL targeting friends of mine. You can rest assured they will be investigated as the foreign funded extortion rackets they truly are should I succeed, but for those who want to support what I'm saying without exposing yourselves, I have five books now which offer a glimpse into the deeper reality of America's struggles and our history, including this final offering, which you can purchase, distribute, and consider.

I'm not a wealthy man. I live off my words and off whatever value people find in these ideas. They took away my job because I was honest, and they kept slandering me in the hope that I would disappear. That's what the system does to people who speak out, but they messed with the wrong guy this time, and I have found there is an insatiable appetite amongst the American people, not to mention the world, for unadulterated truth, and so I simply share what I think and allow you to consider. Even those who disagree will usually admit I'm very direct in what I offer.

I'm told it isn't Presidential to say White people are pretty awesome and we should be proud of ourselves, that Islam is a barbaric religion that won't mesh well with us, that multiculturalism is causing us to have disgust for one another, or that two parents are better than one. But I'm going to say these things and more, not for shock value, but because you deserve a leader who will actually tell you what is true instead of just pretending everything is as good as everything else. You don't have to agree with me, but even if you think I'm the biggest idiot in America, you might just appreciate a real conversation instead of a prepackaged farce.

So, this will be a different campaign, and it will be brash and offensive at times. I know it will also be hurtful, so I want to take a moment to discuss that. I believe in the essential dignity of each human person as a spiritual truth and that each man or woman can find salvation and grace. Even as I talk about our differences, I always acknowledge and celebrate the power of any individual to overcome their challenges. I know there are people who genuinely believe concepts, identities, and affiliations I will speak against who are good people, and whom I may even personally admire. So, with all that, I will say we all have things we do that are less than ideal, myself most certainly included, and understand that if I attack something you do, believe, or act upon, it does not mean I hate you personally. Christians say love the sinner, hate the sin, and if you understand that in my efforts to share what I think is wrong I want to see the betterment of all who are afflicted, then you might better understand why I can be so strident.

I accept that others will come to the table holding their own ideas just as strongly, often in contradiction to my own, and can accept there will be times when we are going to differ. In those times, we have to learn how to push government back, allow free association or dissociation, and understand that living in mutual amity requires both patience and reciprocity: Values both antithetical to the nanny state we're now birthing.

Most Americans accept tolerance uncritically, thinking themselves high minded. I always see it as a cop out where it means you care so little about those around you, you'll simply watch idly as people destroy their own lives just because you don't want to be bothered with the mistakes they're making. We've all been there and had to watch that, but we can't do that anymore at the national level, because it is costing us our country.

So, I want to hear what you think, from letters to the editor to messages on social media. This campaign is for all ages, all parties, and if you really want to see something special, all those who come over to the Republican side and push aside an old, tired, and corrupt party for one that expresses new national vigor and love of the fatherland.

For too long, I think we've let ourselves hold a very narrow view of what is possible, and accepted leadership we knew was corrupt and inadequate. We don't need money to run DC anymore, and this changes when we, the people, take over one of these parties and push our way forward to the front. We've seen how nationalism has already established a beachhead in the GOP, and this party is ripe for the taking. Nationalism, populism, traditionalism and realism are what we need in order to achieve our manifest destiny of American excellence based upon virtue, principle, sound habits, and leadership. We need to slaughter the old sacred cows of false civility and political correctness and make our country truly greater than before.

In some ways, this is the path that we started to take when President Trump upset the natural order of elections. But where he settled into the DC political game, we're not going to make the same mistake. We will remain the movement, will continue the push, and not simply settle. We will put America first, we will call out the ideas we know to be insane, and we're not going to go swimming in the swamp. As my writings demonstrate, I'm very serious about tackling the issues that sustain the corruption, and I will do whatever is required to ensure the American restoration is complete or will die trying. I couldn't launch this campaign if I accepted any less.

As serious as this will be, this should also be a fun campaign and one I want you to make your own. We engage with anyone, talk to everyone, from the far right to the far left, and we reject the idea that anyone is too good or too bad to help retake America from those who have defrauded us all. We want to hear your ideas, your vision, and to encourage you to speak to others. Always call out the lies and hypocrisy and help me ride a groundswell to remove the big faceless actors that constrain us all. This will be a dangerous time, but our Founders always understood that liberty carries a high price and a high personal responsibility.

Most importantly, have a little fun. Campaigns are very long and very challenging, and we have a long way to go. Get your memes rolling, your jokes lined up, and let's see what we can do when we put our minds to it. There will be plenty of serious stuff ahead, as we talk policy, and I don't mean to suggest everything is a joke. Far from it. But we need to keep our balance if we are going to try to something so challenging as liberating America from Washington.

Now that we have covered how to make things happen, let me share with you the big ideas that I plan to feature in the months ahead about how we retake America. Some will likely be very controversial, but they are a starting point from which we can work, and each has been carefully considered as means to address specific problems that destroy our unity, subvert our confidence, or rob from our people.

Immigration and Demography

A country is its people. We are told that nothing matters more than our laws, but the idea that a well-designed charter like our Constitution can somehow magically guarantee America can overcome anything is patently false. Those laws, just like any other, are dependent upon having a population that understands their intent, honors their purpose of balancing liberty with authority, and doesn't seek to play the system for personal or group gain at the expense of society as a whole.

Since 1965, America has been importing people on the wrong basis. To be very clear, I am not saying that every person who has come here has been bad or that none have contributed to our society. Many have. But what I am saying is that whereas America once had an immigration process that offered nothing but opportunity and was largely restricted to people with a similar cultural and heritage background of earlier settlers, a key component to the ease with which they were assimilated and able to blend into the proverbial melting pot, the immigration policy America enacted after the passage of the Hart-Celler Act of 1965 changed everything.

Instead of seeking the best people the world had to offer who shared our values, the decision was made to deliberately select people who had nothing in common with the United States, from areas of the world that practiced hostile religions and were less developed, and who would be chosen randomly from no more likely attribute than their countries of origin no longer wanting them or their desire to leave where they were permitted such a choice. Not only would we welcome them here, but they would be granted an increasingly generous package of welfare benefits, taking resources away from the American people, and once a single member of a family had established permanent residency here, they could form a human chain to bring in others nominally related by blood.

To put in perspective how many people we are talking about, there are now 45 million foreign born US citizens, not to mention millions more in process, and I haven't even mentioned the tens of millions of illegal aliens who add to this number. The census bureau estimates one in eight citizens are now from abroad, which means with the illegals and people in process, as many as one in five or even one in four people in America are not native born. The question I ask you is: At what point does assimilation give way to replacement because there is no way any country can integrate so many people coming in so quickly in a multicultural environment?

Most Republicans frame immigration as a question of border security and law enforcement. They point, rightly, to the sordid practice of human trafficking, drug trafficking, and the use of illegal labor by unscrupulous Americans. We need to combat these. I support not only building a southern border wall, but permanently militarizing our

Southern border and working with Mexico to help them secure their far shorter southern border against future caravans and to interdict drugs coming from Latin America. These are no-brainers despite the Left's opposition, but inasmuch as Americans deserve to be safe from crime, even if each of these actions were enacted, they alone miss the larger problem.

We have too many people here who we can't integrate and as such, America is no longer defining itself, but instead becoming like the Third World countries from whom we receive the most population. Of the ten countries from whom we receive the most people, Mexico is by far the largest, but the other top ten are either Asian, African, or Latino in origin. No one likes to point out the obvious, but people from those regions also make up the three racial blocs most likely to support socialism, welfarism, and to vote for Democrats. You get called a racist for pointing out actual patterns, but who we are bringing into America is making this entire country have a voting habit just like California, a one party state that votes entirely left, pays welfare for legal and illegal immigrants alike, and proudly features sanctuary cities where the invaders are allowed to vote.

We need to be very honest and recognize Democrats see this as a feature of their refusal to have any limitations on open borders or immigration, because the socialist policies they could never persuade America to adopt come naturally to people who lived in parts of the world where such thinking is business as usual. Their egalitarian universalism cares far less about citizenship than control, and so when they see the chance to add Latinos who vote 2/3 of the time, Asians who vote ¾ of the time, and Africans who vote 9/10 of the time for their party, it's a slam dunk they're going to take that offer. If you want to contest those statistics, I encourage you to consult the exhaustive database Pew Research offers and do your own research; it will open your eyes.

Meanwhile, the geniuses at the Republican Party who apparently can't do math offer false platitudes about how legal immigration is great for America. Maybe it was way back when, but as a country that is spiraling upwards of 20 trillion dollars in debt, where crime is rampant in many cities, and where our culture itself is being torn apart into different languages and ghettos, we need to put an immediate halt to these changes and stop bringing in more people. In New York City, election ballots are translated into more than 90 languages. We need a hard stop on new immigrants, and frankly, we probably need to send some refugees and others, like those who have committed criminal acts, back home. I don't care if you call me racist for looking out for the interests of the people who were born here and whose parents and forefathers bestowed this country upon us: We have no inherent obligation to non-citizens, and it's time for a National Republican Party that has the courage to state this obvious truth.

The alternative is we lose America. The single biggest reason I jumped into the race this cycle is as I was crunching the math, I realized we are just one more big amnesty away from America becoming a permanent minority-majority electorate. In the era of identity politics, which is working quite well for the Left despite them revealing their plan too soon, that means a future where the Whites who are already targeted when we speak in our self-interests will be facing a polity that is hostile to us, hostile to American heritage and tradition, hateful of Christianity, and now with a numerical majority and a willingness to use government without any restraint to inflict reparations. You might remember how quickly Obama was able to weaponize the Department of Justice into a totally different animal with money for law enforcement diverted to selected progressive activists for community policing, and you should never doubt these socialists know how to empower their own.

We need to stop this. We need to do it now. We need the Republican Party to take the hard line on immigration, to be realists about demographics, and to begin acting to renew the culture as a source of unity. In subsequent chapters, we'll talk about how we can rein in the media to prevent them from enforcing political correctness and to open up the debate once more, and also how we can encourage the tech giants to do the right thing in honoring our liberties. But this is the one fight we cannot escape.

It is also an issue where President Trump has it wrong. As much as I respect his fight for the Wall and for border security, what he is arguing is just the politically safe subset issue of what is required. That he is going out and saying we need more immigrants than ever just demonstrates he fundamentally doesn't understand the cultural cost of bringing people in here who think differently. Moreover, not only do they begin with a dangerous empathy for state communism, but they also enter a public education system which we know only reinforces the worst progressive ideals. Whatever the economic benefit, the opportunity cost of losing what it means to be American must be far greater. Furthermore, to be entirely honest, we don't need more cheap labor to compete against our employees or impending automation, nor do we need to offset the failures of our education system by importing skilled labor to fill jobs native born Americans will need.

This is one reason why I, unlike any other major American politician, have adopted identity as part of what I defend. It should be obvious that every people are worthy of respect, and Whites are certainly no exception, but I know that Whites through both habit and social resistance, prefer to look at things from a race blind perspective. The problem is that if you do that, it's easy to both become a group that does not enjoy the same protections as any other American, and to overlook what is happening to us today. For the first point, did you know that Whites have no legal protection if fired on a racial basis, unlike every other group in America? We have a built-in systemic prejudice which denies us the same legal protection, not to mention the many cases where the government offers special support or consideration to minorities. You're told we have a meritocracy, and I could live with that, but the reality is quite the opposite. In truth, we have become a targeted class, and as such, I encourage White people everywhere to consider our interest as a group, if only defensively, because we are actively being targeted for diminution by the Left wing which sees us as both unjust and the last obstacle to their goals.

A National Republican Party which could unite Whites to vote in our common interest, which may very well be for a blind meritocracy based on liberty and opportunity, would have the votes still to dominate America and could do away with identity politics of resentment and instead shift the basis to respect and admiration. The Left knows this, fears this, and that's why they paint advocates of positive White identity as perpetual Nazis and a bigger threat to America than serial murderers. Knowing many of the men and women who hold these views, I'll tell you nothing could be further from the truth. These are people who love America, love our history, and love our people as we are – not as who we are supposed to become, and they're ready to be the allies we need to push back if the conservative base is finally ready for a fight to stop replacing America and start restoring these United States. It starts when you say you're proud to be White, and you can and will work with every other group who loves America too.

I know there are millions of people in this country who are not of European origin who feel just the same way, and with a meritocracy that is race realistic in orientation, but honors individuals and their opportunity, we can finally push back with strength and in mutual alliance toward a future that preserves liberty and destroys this cancerous obsession with socialism. We will have the strength to say that no more people can come here, and we will be able to remake our schools, and reclaim our values.

That is the fight I intend to take forward, and I'm ready for every sling they throw at me for speaking this most inconvenient truth. If elected, I will work to see every illegal returned to their country of origin, promise no more amnesties, and to also seek to repatriate as quickly and safely as possible refugees in America to their home lands or safe third countries more appropriate for their cultural habit. Moreover, in the interests of doing this humanely, I will support a hardline against those who harbor illegals or hire them, and will use every power of the law to end sanctuary cities. I will refuse to recognize any votes from non-citizens in this country and will work toward voting reforms that require identification that clearly shows a potential voter's citizenship status.

We have been invaded and one of our parties is shamefully holding the door open in what is an act of treason. We must call this what it is, and demand that our political process returns its loyalty to the people of America, and to all our citizens. In this, there will be a place for all legal citizens, but we will not give one inch on this issue, including to the many local governments which are breaking the law through enabling this ongoing invasion. It is an act of sedition and I argue legal officials working for local governments who do not actively cooperate with ICE and other agencies should be held personally liable for what is a criminal act.

The Democrats don't care about our security or integrity because they would be just as glad to see other people replace you. They don't care that the billions they spend on social services for these people could pay for health care or drug rehabilitation for millions of Americans. The Republicans care, but not enough to risk being called racists or give up the cheap labor they have cynically exploited for as long as I can remember. But as a nationalist, I care because I know we cannot take care of our people as well as we should if we're investing so much time, money, and energy into people who might be very good people, but whose problems cannot become our primary concern. I don't blame the people for wanting to be Americans, but I blame our corrupt leadership instead for taking advantage of the outsider as a wedge against us, the citizens.

We would literally save hundreds of billions of dollars that could go to so many better uses, and we'd also have safer cities and the ability to begin working toward greater cultural unity if we cut off the tap. We could and should push for universal use of English as the American language, and to stop all social welfare to non-citizens. We would see fewer drugs on our streets, and we would stop this idea that the American majority can be bred out through immigration. It's very harsh to say it that way, but I believe that a strategy of population replacement is precisely what we're facing, just as the Europeans are with their own corrupt governments and how they have taken in millions from the Muslim world, and that sort of elitism is precisely what I guarantee we will stop.

Corruption and Connivance

It's almost impossible to know where to begin this category, but it's equally difficult to pretend any attempt to fix Washington has any chance of success without admitting the whole government reeks of corruption. It's never been far from my mind that nearly all the richest counties in America directly ring the District of Columbia, and public service has never been so lucrative. It is a bought town where people openly trade influence like some sort of stock exchange where our citizens are treated as the commodity.

As best I can tell, the offenses run in a few basic directions. There is basic graft where people go ahead and sell policy and information to the highest bidder, a perfectly respectable profession down there in the capital which we need to rein in heavily. There are also those within government who believe their authority far transcends both statute and intent, who essentially use their status to make policy rather than follow the expressed will of the people. We've seen much more of that Deep State variety of subversion of late, and it should be troubling.

These last few years, I've watched the current administration struggle mightily to accomplish their intentions because when anyone reform minded comes along, they end up tied in a tangle of red tape and are led in every direction but that of truth. Trump brought in DC swamp dwellers to help, and now the whole place has the familiar odor of alligators and snakes. I think this was a mistake, and that you can't really fix DC from the inside.

To that end, one thing I believe very strongly that must be done is whomever comes into government to fix Washington can't be from the system itself. While I am sure there are excellent people there in some quarters working to sustain a broken edifice, my basic inclination is to think the people there are too close to the problem. If elected, frankly, I don't intend to spend all my time there either, because it becomes a bubble that insulates and isolates policy makers from the real people who live in the heartland and hinterland alike. I'd rather work with people who live in the actual world instead of that fantasy land, and if Congress doesn't like that, well it wouldn't be the first time a kitchen cabinet was needed to disrupt the cartel.

Furthermore, I strongly suspect a good number of our Congress are irredeemably corrupt, and I say this as an utterly nonpartisan statement. It's very lucrative to deliver the goods to the right interest groups, whether a Republican or Democrat, and as a co-equal branch of government, I think it appropriate to begin looking at why certain policies continue getting support despite the clearly expressed will of the American people against them. One obvious example is how we never seem to get out of any wars, and as I've been watching the Congress literally try to punish the current President for wanting to return our troops home to safety and for our own security, I cannot help but wonder what foreign lobbies and defense contractors are lining their pockets. Consider me a cynic when it comes to the willingness of our representatives to make use of our government for personal benefit, but I think some discussion on these issues and tracing the dollar trails might prove quite revealing.

The Federal bureaucracy is a nightmare and should be ashamed of itself. We've watched the FBI try to fix elections, the CIA involved in drug trafficking, the EPA overreach into declaring puddles to be lakes, and I could go on for hours. What we need to do is figure out why we have so many agencies, rein in their powers, and probably the only way we can actually accomplish this is to begin cutting agencies. Considering that we're now more than twenty trillion dollars in debt, I think it's time the government largess be reduced, and we can start with everyone who has abused their office.

I'm committed to far greater transparency moving forward in what our security state has done, so look for a declassification of a number of different areas. While I understand actions would have been undertaken with what was perceived with the best interests of the country at the time, a process of review and analysis by the people themselves is needed, and so you're going to see me try to kick down some heavily locked doors. I would expect the Deep State to declare war upon this movement I'm launching in response, because it's easier to silence one voice than to allow the truth to come out, and I'm not naïve enough to think my life is so valuable someone might not try to take it from me. It's sad we live in such a corrupt country, but ask Seth Rich about that.

As a general rule, I believe in decentralization. Power returned to the most local level capable of performing a government service permits the greatest transparency and choice. I think we've usurped far too many powers to the national level, and we've undoubtedly obliterated the Constitutional restraint clearly articulated within the Tenth Amendment about reserved powers. A conversation is necessary about just what powers should be kept at the highest level, and beyond that, the Federal government needs to reduce its own authority and oversight back to the States and the People, respectively. In many areas, I don't believe a one size fits all solution works for America, and getting back to allowing different regions to act in their own habit will probably help alleviate some political tension.

But, one place I differ strongly is in working to create a common culture and to ensure our education system stops its current cultural jihad against America. We need a common language, a common set of voting laws, basic education about citizenship, and it would be incredibly helpful if common values were demonstrated. We need to push toward a service-based model of government instead of one where financial benefit predominates, and we need to insist our public sector works always, solely, and strictly for the benefit of the American people. We are not globalists, owe no sovereignty to the UN or any other institution, and will not try to satisfy some cosmopolitan impulse.

I've become very skeptical about our current manifestation of democracy because it seems to me to be a very easy system to buy. As a populist and nationalist, I inherently agree government should serve the people, but this ping-pong version of policy isn't working for anyone. It only creates a schizophrenic policy agenda where nothing gets done, that encourages people buying offices, and provides an illusion of choice that masks a reality of well-heeled interests purchasing both parties for the areas they care about, usually those that involve the most expenditure, while the partisans bicker over social issues that don't have the same financial import. That's why you see everyone agree to fund international security even while they refuse to protect our own borders.

George Washington warned America that political parties would lead to this outcome, and it's part of the reason why I'm declaring war on both parties. I encourage others to run alongside me to unseat every incumbent within the Republican Party as the people who serve in Washington have made jokes of the conservative base for years, pissing on everything we ever elected them to accomplish. We don't need these people – we need fresh blood.

I don't know if Democrats will care very much what I think, but I would recommend they do the same. I realize our very partisan disagreements will make life difficult, but at least a fresh crop of people might not rehearse the same old themes. If people from the other side are willing to meet on the basis of how we can benefit our American people while maintaining respect for liberty and authority, and without forcing equality upon us, I'm ridiculously pragmatic in how I think about policy and will look to forge a consensus that works to the best realistic outcome. It's important to be able to work with good people, but sadly, these are in short supply in DC.

We need to rethink how government works, and I cannot help but note we're coming up on the two hundred fiftieth anniversary of our country. We live in a different world than the Founders could have ever imagined, and it seems like we should maybe look at their timeless wisdom in defending and strengthening the core liberties that have made the American experiment work, but also re-examine how government was structured seeing how we can all admit current institutions fall far short of reflecting the public interest. We need to figure out how to combat the corrupting influence of money, how to better balance centralization versus autonomy, and to place certain authority and values above these constant disputes lest we tear ourselves apart. We're on a path for self-destruction with our current disputes, and no one will like where that goes.

A civil war would be very nasty and involve the death of millions. I write on it frequently and have done more than one or two interviews on this question. There are times people on the fringes think about it and imagine the best of all possible outcomes in simply undoing all that doesn't work and having the reset to make America. I'm no exception to this, yet, the reason it hasn't happened is because enough people have realized that long before any potential benefit, the human and material cost would be utterly devastating, perhaps even worse than the incessant theft and corruption of our capital. So, decent folk watch more angrily each day, and keep trying new attempts at reform, but patience is wearing thin out here, and the attempts to remake America into things groups will not abide is a real threat. Probably on both sides.

It's important we get real about the problems in front of us, and the swindlers who are just working for their own benefit have shown they either don't know or don't care how dangerous the territory we've entered has become. The media simply continues goading us along as they throw out slurs and falsehoods, and they enable people to commit dereliction of duty whether elected or serving as mandarins within the permanent bureaucracy. It isn't right, and it needs to change. As austere as my vision might be in these areas, it will be far better than the cost of continuing to pretend the problems will just go away.

So, I offer a new national consensus based on virtue and looking out for our people. I promise firm leadership and that we will be cutting away much of what is bad. It will be incredibly contentious and ugly, and there will undoubtedly be good people caught amongst the bad as we fix the system. It will require decisive use of executive authority, and frankly, investing more power into our military as trusted arbiters to carry on key functions as we unmask the failures of Federal law enforcement, security agencies, and other institutions. I cannot say more than that because we don't know what we will find, but we can share the results, and recognize that corruption against the republic is a crime not against the parties, but rather the people themselves and I would hope we can get past this useless showmanship.

I suspect we won't right away, however, which is why, to beat corruption, we need a new government. We need you, and we need you to vote out whomever was there before. It's a truism that while people hate Congress, they usually like their representative, but I hate to share that in most cases, they're part of the problem. If it helps, think upon it this way: We all need a new start some time, and public service isn't meant to be forever. As someone who has walked away from politics several times in life and will surely do so again one day, I can imagine few things so miserable as imaging this to be all there is in life, for as important as these struggles are, one loses perspective when too close to the problem. That's why I live in the rural expanse of Maine, because it reminds me that the world doesn't have to be like DC, but the people there have forgotten that lesson. We must now teach them anew.

Culture and Censorship

Politics exists downwind of culture. Culture is how we visually and viscerally assert and seek out truth, but America has been sorely and deliberately divided in this area, which is why our fractious political discord has resulted. We cannot agree on a truth, on core values, or who should lead and how. As such, we have come to mistrust one another, hatred runs rampant, and we hide this disgust beneath a thin veneer of practiced restraint which we sometimes call tolerance. In each book I write, I always remind the reader that tolerance merely means caring so little for your fellow person you'll allow them to do anything, and America has somehow delved so deeply into this self-indulgent fantasy that we have become a hundred little separated tribes.

It goes without saying that we need to put things back together, and my preferred formulation looks something like 1950 with a return to the traditional family, with more commonly expressed roles that people followed, enough wealth for children to be raised by their parents, and a happier aesthetic. I close my eyes and I can almost picture it, but rest assured, I know we can't just go back, and it won't be that simple. For better or worse, I'm a realist, and we live in country where my dream is probably someone else's nightmare. But, I do think we can have a conversation about certain commonalities, agree the present needs to be looking out for the future, admit families matter a great deal, and see that there is a real cost to this insane march toward forced diversity: Loss of unity.

This is why I started by saying America doesn't need more people, because those of us already here can hardly agree on anything. That much should be plainly obvious, but we're not even allowed to assert this basic truth because the people who run our culture have weaponized it against reality. One isn't allowed to use truth with a capital "T" because that might offend someone's feelings, and the snowflake mentality which seems to those less aware as a strange form of adult infantilism is, in fact, an incredibly astute form of subversion known as cultural Marxism. It weaponizes language and sentiment to create division, all in the service of trying to realize essential equality, and has been an elite project for many generations now throughout the West.

They set us against one another, destroy all sources of authority outside the state, and simply watch as we self-destruct presenting an ever-growing government as the solution. Sometimes, it is a bigger bureaucracy in DC. Other times, they recommend unelected international bodies like the corrupt United Nations. But without fail, the people who own our media and who sit in comfortable tenured positions seek to destroy beauty and authority within our culture, attacking all which is healthy and reaffirming, and encouraging anger and resentment. They are the true enemy of the people, and though we might have to fight one another as partisans and may have to remove people who have been brought here only as pawns in their larger and more heartless game, my hatred is reserved for those who know better and choose to divide America anyway.

In case there is any doubt, I want to be explicitly clear that I see the corporate media as the enemy of the people. I have watched for years as they lie time and again, presenting false narratives as they destroy good people who speak up for restraint or morality. I also hate their allies in these groups who go around as censors and judges, pushing people into mobs before social guillotines who print just a few headlines and destroy lives. They think themselves our betters, and that they get to pass moral judgment even as they simply sell their souls out to destroy everything around them.

I am proud this will be a social media driven campaign where we are going to go around the talking heads that treat the people like morons and who lecture us about what we are supposed to think. Should I succeed, we're going to break up those media conglomerates and return ownership of the media to locals, to Americans, and no longer allow them to create these false echo chambers. You can't really appreciate what they do until you've been in the crucible, so I will try to explain for public benefit. They pick a story, a narrative, and then write a hundred variations on a single theme. They exert pressure with activists who, though never large in number, are made to appear like some huge outcry, and then they force submission.

Talk to them and they lie. Ignore them and they slander. Dispute them and they run. Because it's not about truth or justice, but rather about a story they want to always tell which is that America is bad, and they know better than you do how to run this and every other country. The media and their friends in the colleges wield guilt like scalpels causing self-doubt, while they push envy in the less intelligent and false altruism in the more privileged. They distort and destroy, and no one ever calls them out when they make things up because they're afraid. I can't guarantee how big this campaign will get, but I've made it my life's work to fight them because of how they slandered me and my family.

Unfortunately, it's getting harder to fight back. As you will have no doubt observed, we now have new things like Newsguard and we see community standards changing everywhere to try to hide the dissent. You might have noticed how comment sections disappear, and how every story on YouTube first lists CNN. Big technology has gotten into bed with big media and they are trying to shape the narrative by hiding independent voices and suppressing dissenting ideas. They claim to be meeting popular demand, but in reality, they're responding to the same activists who dominate corporate media, who are pushing away your right to hear a different side of the story.

We need to work quickly if we are going to ensure free speech isn't just an anachronism in America. I support making tech and media companies directly liable for not allowing expression of free speech, and to push back against this horrible international idea of a social media score being used like a credit report. The conformity that would force would be chilling, and this Chinese wet dream is antithetical to the core of what it means to be American even though the eggheads in Silicon Valley seem oblivious to this. I will make sure we stop the selective targeting, deplatforming, and definancing that is happening to people who hold nonconforming views.

For those who aren't in the weeds like I've been these last few years, you might not understand all that, so the simplest way I can explain this is that people are being "un-personed" for their political views. For example, when I lost my job for speaking out about Islam and for the rights of White people, did you know my wife was banned from being able to raise money publicly on most major platforms such as Patreon and GoFundMe to help raise funds for treating her disease? Do you think that was appropriate? I'll bet you had no clue things like this happen, but people who offend the politically correct consensus are branded, hidden away from the world, and continually targeted for economic and social destruction as well as ongoing harassment. I know story after story of people who, just for supporting traditional identity, or being Christians, and other innocuous offenses, have had their lives ruined. No one cares about these statistics, because the cruel media paints these people as having done it to themselves.

I was told after the fact that they came to destroy me because they thought it was a good time for a story about Maine designed to push people into supporting more diversity. They decided we weren't good enough the way we were, as hardworking Americans, and needed to become more like how they live in the big city, how the elites want us to live where we can't choose our friends but have to be like everyone else. This is the world of equality they imagine, where they choose for everyone how we have to live, and that petty totalitarianism creeps ever more deeply into our lives even as its biggest fans live as clear hypocrites above and beyond their own purported rules. These people are bullies who use words instead of weapons, and I know from the simple wisdom my father taught me, the only way to beat people like this is to punch them in the mouth.

To that end, I want to share that I believe in free speech as an absolute value, and I would fight for people to say things that irritate the hell out of me. I certainly believe in standards and in arguing back, but I think that makes America work better than this idea that we should somehow be tactfully silent about things that are true and uncomfortable. I basically have come to make a living in talking about areas that are incredibly sensitive, and while I try to do it with grace and humility, I know it doesn't take much spin to make me look like a heartless bastard.

Whatever else we must do, I think we need to reset our society to a basis built upon truth, that is cognizant of our inherent nature, and recognizes while we can change and alter some things, a happy future is one in which we live according to our natural dictates. This is not a new idea. Sir Francis Bacon, one of our earliest modern scientists saw this clearly when he stated that "Nature to be commanded, must be obeyed." I've often described what I see happening in the larger social scene as a war against nature and reality, where we are forced to treat up as down and vice versa, and I think people are sick of this. We're pressed into so many roles and made to regurgitate so many things we simply know aren't true for fear of giving offense. The reality is life isn't always fair, sometimes we are going to say tough and occasionally cruel things, and we need to deal with things as they truly are rather than how we would wish they might be.

Only from that basis can we reconnect our increasingly disparate cultures into one tapestry that might hold together for enough of us to be preserved. There are days when I wonder if it is even still possible, especially as we have forces working against our success with every moment of the news cycle, but I want to believe there are still commonalities from which we can build. In spite of my strong views on culture and tradition, I enjoy talking with people who think differently than I do when it is a substantive and sincere conversation, and that's where it starts.

Consider me, if you like, the voice of unrepentant traditional America. I'm a White guy who knows his history, owns it, and is proud of it. I accept Christ as my personal savior, believe men and women actually were happier with the old roles of provider and wife, and I live according to these precepts. Millions are like me, and even though we're daily degraded, we are coming back up with a new generation who will not be cowed by false guilt. We believe money isn't the answer to everything, that selfishness has its limits, and that families need to rise above individual whims once more. I don't want to have to see degeneracy every five seconds and doubt others do also, but I can admit others may make different choices if we can agree upon common rules for the public space. Is that a starting point to move past the culture wars? You tell me.

But the one thing I won't do is back down, because as I've written in many places as well, the Right-thinking people of this country have been coerced into silence for fear of social and economic penalties for too long. By now, you would think people have realized the silent majority is a thing. But we're not going to be silent any more, and we're going to demand respect for our views, and stop the war against our history and heritage. You can disagree, but you will not erase us, and we will not let you tell these lies unopposed.

Now, I'm realistic enough to know taking such positions may lead us into a fight we cannot avoid. I reckon that a better choice than continuing along silently in support of lies that have become commonly accepted as facts. This is why I tell people the two most important issues are demographics and culture: Because our future will be determined by our people and our choice to adhere to either truth, or fantasy. For a long time, we haven't had anyone say that. It seems that we've been lost in the minutiae, but struggles like this really do matter, and we just can't submit anymore. We compromised for years to try to have peace, and all that brought us was progressive politically correct insanity.

So now, we don't compromise our beliefs. We will defend marriage, traditional values, love of our country, and indeed, Western Civilization and our proud history and ethnicity. I am honored to take up the sword and shield for all these causes, and feel unconstrained by false guilt and have no fear of the lies that will be told. I think people are ready for someone who speaks openly and honestly and doesn't mouth false platitudes. I don't pretend everyone thinks what the Right believes, but for those who do, know that I will try to faithfully articulate our case, admitting that I will always be imperfect in my own failings, but perhaps inspired to do better by fighting for this cause.

People who believe … find their better selves. It's strange to think, but I'll close this chapter with gratitude for my enemies. They forced me to be better, to try harder, and to care more. The process of losing sixty pounds sucked, but I've never felt better or thought more clearly. I've never been optimistic or hopeful, and to live a life with purpose with love of my people, even those who have some things wrong, is a life of excellence to which any can and all should seek their own path forward.

Don't let the liars in the media and the charlatans and censors keep you from finding and speaking the truth. I know I won't.

Meritocracy and Opportunity

Most Americans seem to want to live in a nominal meritocracy. By that, I mean we want a country where a person is treated as an individual without regard to any external characteristic and is judged on the basis of actions, character, and any achievements. Many Americans pretend we already have such a system, and while there is certainly mobility (in some cases) for those who work hard, we've seen backsliding against this system for a long time now. Much of this, as usual, has to do with the Left.

Their obsession with equality and the desire to equalize outcomes has led them to support state intervention in numerous areas for many different reasons. The problem is that subsidizing people comes with a great cost in that people come to expect the government will serve as caretaker for them and such paternalistic policies create whole groups who basically exist to realize benefits from the state. Instead of actively participating in government as free citizens, they become hostage to the benefits they accrue and simply vote for their maintenance and expansion. Welfare voters are very real, and while I agree there are times a safety net is needed for the security of our people, it is very damaging to create permanent classes who subsist at this level.

What makes it worse is this economic welfarism has been coupled with the explicit embrace of politics by division, especially by race, and is a process nearly a half century into expansion. This gets covered far more extensively in some of my other writings, but the Great Society and the Civil Rights Act did not seek to just equalize voting and other rights for minorities with the majority, but rather it envisioned a system where the state would serve as caretaker and shepherd for certain groups, especially those from minority racial groups, and to provide them special legal sanction, certain protections, and advantageous standing when it came to consideration for opportunities. Think of affirmative action as the government holding its thumb down on the majority to help the minority, which inherently comes at the expense of even the best performing majority individual student.

Politics doesn't exist in a vacuum. When you give a special sanction to one group, even if it is genuinely intended to correct a perceived historical slight, an ideology is created whereby the group advantaged by that sanction comes to see themselves as being owed special privilege or recompense for historical wrongdoing. What began with reparations, will blossom into a fully-fledged apparatus to seek the wholesale reconstruction of America, all because well-intended people failed to perceive an ideology of victimization and seeking power through stoking perpetual envy and an inferiority/superiority dynamic. This progressive ideal has taken over the Democrats, and it is why they are utterly incapable of defending meritocracy, because they are torn apart by indoctrinated guilt in half their party and righteous indignation within what they call the "coalition of the ascendant." Such strong feelings of anger and resentment do not easily give way to reason and restraint, and when you see how vitriolic their rhetoric has become, you need to know this is the root.

A recurring theme in my writing is that many of the politically incorrect issues we discuss are not considered with the right weight. As with race and political organization, it's often the case that the two sides differ in such a manner that one side pretends the issue is nonexistent, which is a mythology of the Right that it wants to believe but which requires a great deal of hypocrisy and deliberate self-delusion to maintain. Meanwhile, the Left has come to believe race means everything and that the majority has a moral mandate to surrender our country over to any who are outside the majority who make a claim. This applies to all manner of groups, ranging from minorities to newly arrived migrants, regardless of legal status, because they are socially just. That is patently absurd as well, that the people who were born here should simply surrender total power and the direction of the country to the newest arrivals. As is usually the case, the real way to understand the problem is to see that race is real, relevant enough to discuss, and important enough to serve as a factor, but that it cannot be the only way to address the questions we have to face.

Politics rewards people who draw bold contrasts and speak in clear moral language. I often do this myself with policy positions because no one would listen to something banal and boring that wanders into the weeds of wonkdom. But with issues of identity, the only way we can even hope to co-exist without realizing all my most dire predictions is with a degree of sensitivity that is rooted in honesty and patience. We need to find the balance where we can respect the differences of the individual, and hold people to a common universal standard on that basis, but be very honest that people also have group identities which cannot be completely left behind, and these have consequences as well.

I state quite clearly in many places that when you commit to replacing the existing American population makeup with a million plus new people each year from the Third World, you're going to end up with a Third World country. I believe part of this is because our different genetic backgrounds lead us to look at the world differently, and we can no more help this than we can change what color eyes we have. I also think culture plays a huge role, and that bringing people in who come from a world where corruption and nepotism are the norm does not strengthen meritocracy in the aggregate. Instead, they decide based upon their eminently logical experience who will serve their interest, and between that analysis and an education system which actively encourages this sort of division, the new Americans gravitate leftward at an eighty percent clip. (This applies even more strongly to the children of Third World immigrants, possibly because the educational system has greater opportunity to indoctrinate.)

Of course, partisans on the Left pompously proclaim this is the arc of justice in history bending in their direction, but the more logical amongst us would just note they're gaming democracy by playing groups off one another. In its simplest terms, after centuries of trying to shift America from a state based on individual opportunity to a state-based form of socialism, the Democrats realized the easier way to accomplish their goal was to change who were Americans. The quickest way to their new America was new people, so they set up a system without any public accountability, where anyone would be taken and where they would be promoted as the new better Americans.

You need only watch media or any commercial to see how constant and relentless the propaganda is. Watch ten commercials and you'll see every minority painted as funny, confident, and successful. You'll see White women pushed toward their strong arms, and you'll see White men presented as nerdy dolts or foils. In a country which is still sixty percent majority, it's funny how shows, media, and marketing all beat this theme with a constant drum beat, which is not one of achievement and individual excellence, but a deliberate effort to demoralize the majority into surrendering our status.

It is your birthright to inherit what your parents left you. This is a universal truth of human civilization, but throughout America and the western world, we see our people voluntarily surrendering that inheritance because of an artificially induced moral crisis that leads us to have no faith in ourselves. This is a deliberate construction of a cultural leadership that wants you to hate yourself, to feel guilt, and that uses political correctness to both mask their population replacement strategy and to punish people who speak out against it. I know, because they call me a white supremacist for merely pointing out the reality of this strategy, and because I believe the people born here should lead here – which I've accepted on the meritocratic basis which White people have solely and uniquely implemented.

If we're really so bad, why is it that we're the only people who welcome others to our home countries? You don't see China admitting millions of foreigners, nor India, nor any non-White majority nation. They look out for their own, which is what nations are supposed to do – represent their actual people, not some idealized externality. But our obsession with equality and thinking there is a system that can transcend our basic biology – which happens not just with race, but with gender and other attributes – might prove our downfall because it just doesn't work. It's not real.

What is real is that we are different, and for us to get along, we really do need one culture and one set of rules. We can talk about race, about grievances, which are a two-way street, and try to move forward. I think such conversations are more easily accomplished when we don't have a rising group being deliberately groomed to be larger each generation and radicalized against the majority. I don't think the Left can stop this, however, which is why I argue for such draconian measures on immigration, because I know our traditional value of meritocracy will not survive in a majority-minority America. Maybe it could have in some theoretical realm, which I doubt, but I'm certain after sixty years of Marxism in the schools and universities, what we actually see on the Left with promises of reparations, justice, and redistribution is precisely what they will offer because it's what the minority population overwhelmingly votes to support. It's rational for the short-term, but suicide for our nation in the long term.

So, here's my counter-offer to anyone who will listen. Let's try a true meritocracy and see what happens. If I'm honest about the systemic factors before the 1960's, we probably never had one, as the majority did have certain benefits, and I can own that. But now, we live in a world where race doesn't have to mean everything, where maybe we can move back toward the 90's consensus of being able to laugh at everyone and talk about anyone without such militancy, and we could have laws that are the same for everyone.

In terms of politics, this means getting rid of gerrymandered districts for minorities, or any special consideration in schools, and that any discrimination laws be applied to all races or none. I believe we should also eliminate hate laws, because the act of a crime is the hatred which should be punished on the specific intent, rather than this creeping effort to criminalize speech and thought, which should permit people to advocate for free association or dissociation. I don't want or think it healthy to force all

Americans to interact accordingly to predetermined formulae, where we need to hire a certain number from each group, and I'm fine with people who choose to keep to their own of any and every group so long as they obey a common set of laws and act with civility and dignity toward others. That's a realistic outcome that is achievable, and it's what I will fight for as my pledge for all American citizens, of every racial background, and I will make myself available to listen to those who have a different experience than I do.

Frankly, I think my embrace of my own racial identity allows me to better and more authentically interact with minorities because I can admit we are different, and that things are not so simple as just being individuals who will always draw the same conclusions given a common problem to solve. So, I will not simply surrender unquestioningly to the idea they're right and the majority is wrong. I have a positive perception of America and the civilization which birthed our country, so I start from that basis, and offer a chance to forge a new path forward which lessens identity politics.

I'll admit my own skepticism that it can be done. It's easier for the Left to just scream that I'm a racist to scare people away from listening, and for the Right to run and hide as they always do from that false charge. It's a funny and very real thing that minorities themselves do not usually engage in this pantomime drama, but it is a uniquely White phenomenon to signal so hard for a system above the reality of people. That isn't lost on me, and if you read what I say with an urge to criticize, consider first whether what I'm saying rings true or not before signaling conformity with what you've been told you must believe.

In a similar but hopefully less controversial vein, I feel the same way about the relationship between men and women and much of what I applied about cultural Marxists programming races against one another applies to the battle between men and women, more within the White community than otherwise. I have a traditional view of gender roles in what I personally prefer, but I also do not expect everyone to conform to those expectations even though I speak to them, and within this same framework of meritocracy, every woman will have equal opportunity and legal protection.

That said, I think it's important and necessary to conclude this chapter by admitting whatever we might wish to be true, while we live as individuals and that governs our existence, the family is and shall forever remain the basic social unit because it does take a man and a woman to create, sustain, and grow new life. We are a part of nature, not apart from nature, I believe nature knows best that a father and a mother make for the happiest child. And I hope through both policy and persuasion to prompt a new age in America where the family centered life comes back to the front as a legitimate means to build a stronger and happier future for parents, partners, and children alike.

We've been a very selfish country for a very long time, and I wonder if the reason we're so messed up doesn't go back to children who came up learning more from schools, television, and the internet than from their families. We internalized that money and status matters more than blood and the people closest to us and were congratulated for making choices based on that premise, but we've never had more people feel disconnected and disaffected. It's something we need to fight, to reconnect to our fellow citizens in an authentic way far beyond what social media allows, and it's a national conversation I hope to lead.

I take the position I do because it can't happen when half the population feels guilt, and the other half feels resentment. We need to find unity, to find a basis upon which we can agree to disagree and to also work together, and it's going to be choppy for a while. But where I think we can and should start is to look at how this corrupt system came into being, and to begin unmaking those institutions which have set us against one another.

History suggests nothing brings separated people back together more quickly than a common cause against a mutual enemy. And we need to declare a war here in America, against our wicked state and the thieves and liars who have neglected all our people for so very long. Because the only thing Americans agree upon anymore is how badly we're being screwed by our own government, and in that, I could not agree more heartily.

Banking and Interest

A Republican isn't supposed to say this, but I hate banks and I hate money. Perhaps there has been a strange fusion of my Swarthmore education and my Christian social ethics here, but when I look at how readily people surrender their beliefs, their friendships, and their energy to the pursuit of wealth, I cannot help but feel disgusted at how quickly so many abandon or discard what they once treasured. Money makes people behave differently, and maybe this is why despite my learning, I've never consciously sought to be a wealthy man. That does not seem the path to happiness, and yet, we have perhaps accepted such as our national pastime because it is a least common denominator that minimizes other disputes.

I understand money is inherently just a tool, and like anything else, it's up to people how they prioritize its accumulation in their own lives. I know plenty of poor people who have terrible habits and attitudes, and a number of very kindly and generous people with wealth. And vice-versa, so I don't judge people based primarily on what they own, but I know so many others do, and I feel like we're pushed toward that sort of society by people who control so much wealth that functionally they treat us all as their playthings.

One cannot seriously study the history of the past few centuries without noting the influence of money, banks, and bankers. In an age which valued learning more highly, it was commonly remarked that all wars were banker wars, and I look to people like Lord Rothschild who once accurately commented in England that it did not matter who controlled the government nearly so much as who owned the currency. He understood that shaping the market impacted the economic reality of every human being in the country, and that in as much as we imagine our government to be sovereign, no political actor or movement can exist outside of the economic purview of those who manage our larger financial network.

Here in the United States, that is the Federal Reserve. For the last decade, we've seen a growing awareness in America that the Fed is not the quiet background actor they want us to believe they are. Many of you will remember the massive bailout in 2007 where trillions of dollars in liquidity were created out of thin air to bail out banks and people who were betting on derivatives and other foolish gambles on Wall Street at the same time the taxpayers were made to bail them out and so many people lost either their homes or a lifetime of equity trapping them in place, with our government rushing on a bipartisan basis to help the fat cats but not the poor people who suffered the real consequences.

Perhaps you remember the infamous phrase regarding the bank bail-out in which banks were described as being "too big to fail." That is, banks had become so large that if even one of them failed, the United States would be plunged into third-world level economic straits. Up until 1994, regulations made it difficult for a bank to exist in many States at once. As a result, the size of most banks was limited to a single state.

You might also recall that prior to 1994, the fees banks levied for most things were considerably lower than today. This was changed by the Riegle-Neal Interstate Banking and Branching Efficiency Act of 1994. What followed was a breathtaking series of mergers and acquisitions both within states and across state lines so that we wound up with just a handful of banks holding 80% of all deposit accounts. Though these mega-banks turned more profit, without effective competition they have run roughshod over our citizens in myriad ways.

But in 2007, the issue at hand was that banking practices had artificially inflated housing prices beyond people's ability to pay, so they tried to keep the bubble growing by issuing all manner of loans, including loans for more than the value of the property, with zero down-payment, and even at zero interest for the first couple of years before the rates exploded. These loans were packaged in numerous ways and resold in bulk, with many banks and even retirement funds holding them. But then, the inevitable happened.

Anyone familiar with personal income statistics in the United States knows that the number of people who can afford the mortgage payment on a house costing $200k, $300k or $500k is minuscule. With downward wage pressure from both legal and illegal immigrants and the country still suffering from the dot-com crash, as soon as the rates on adjustable rate mortgages made their first jump, the foreclosures started rolling in. And lenders quickly discovered that they couldn't sell the homes for enough to pay off the loans.

After 18 million families lost their homes, foreclosure rates finally dropped to historic norms. Yet even now, more than a decade after the crisis, and long after brokers have spent their commissions, 10% of home owners owe more on their home than it is worth. But while ordinary American citizens were losing their homes and struggling under artificially created debt to enrich a handful at the top of a financial scheme, our Federal government bailed out these "too big to fail" banks by incurring debt that our children will be forced to pay in taxes.

This was a trans-partisan issue. I was there with my friends on the Right chanting to audit the Fed, and I went to visit the people in the streets on the Left who tried to Occupy Wall Street. Both had a piece of the truth, which is that usurious lending practices have destroyed the sovereignty of America, and that the banking system which exists does not serve the purposes of the people. The so-called "creature from Jekyll Island," drafted in a secret assembly by rich oligarchs and plutocrats late in the night, has never been there to serve the American people, but instead is the cynical means by which a few people have accumulated so much wealth as to functionally run this world.

Imagine, if you can, creating money out of thin air. Once called inflation, now called quantitative easing, that's what the central bank does, and it helps who it wants by reducing the rate by which money is introduced into the economy, to go as low as even zero or in some cases, to offer negative rates (to pay banks to loan money!) at which money is fabricated and then introduced into the economy. How just is it ... that the wealthiest banks get billions for free, which they loan to the rest of us at a healthy profit margin? How fair is it that our government pays interest to these same people to print the same currency we hold in our wallets and checking accounts?

If you answered that this sounds like a ridiculous scam, you and I are of one mind, and it's one to which more Americans are waking up to each day. Much of the 19th Century was fought against the creation of such a bank, and it is due primarily to this issue that I reckon Andrew Jackson our greatest President ever because he survived an assassination attempt after which he personally bludgeoned his failing assailant to go on to kill the Bank of the United States, the spiritual predecessor of the Fed which was only sapping the wealth of our country to the control of the moneylenders.

There are a number of excellent books written on this topic, which make very clear that the Federal Reserve is a privately held entity over which the government exercises only very limited oversight. There are institutions which own stock in this, and no one has ever been permitted to know who these owners are or how much their money is worth. We do know they own, in association with other sovereign banks that have similar ownership interests like the Bank of England, most of the global gold supply. We also know countries whose banks aren't part of this, or who try to do oil transactions in currency other than U.S. dollars are often targeted for revolution and overthrow, as was the case with Iraq, Libya, Syria, and Iran. Do your own research if you don't believe me.

But what we also know is they've been destroying the wealth of the American people by inflating our currency for over a century now. When you see old advertising from way back when and that everything cost a nickel or a dime, what gets lost is that it doesn't inherently cost more to make things today. Instead, your money simply buys less, and that's why the American people have been cheated of their wealth, because all this free money and interest the banks are making inflates the money supply, reducing the purchasing power of your dollar. The simplistic minded think the answer is to give people more money, but those who really study this understand that doesn't help unless you stop the people at the top from stealing from all of us.

We're told finance is very complicated and economics uses jargon to conceal what is a simple scam. It's a con game where fiat currency, money that has no intrinsic value, is printed at whatever rate is most sustainable, and where it only gains value by what we give up or trade for its growth. For the people who run the banks, they get it for free and skim off the top. For us working people, we slave our lives away to get just a few dollars which are worth less every moment we hold them. This is what we get from the Federal Reserve, and why I want to see it ended. I want to see power to print money returned to our US Treasury as Kennedy was starting to do before they had him killed, and want to be very clear the people whom I fear most are the people who run these institutions. They do kill to keep their secret safe, and yet, America cannot be liberated when we are held in bondage to such debt holders.

I propose a simple beginning to test my case. We should begin by auditing the Fed and opening up their books to see who owns what, what has been done, and let the people with greater knowledge than you or I see how they've managed our economy. They would claim they try to be good stewards preventing too much inflation or the deflation of not trying to have constant maintained economic growth. Now, I personally believe the latter is impossible, and that's why we are drowning amidst $22 trillion in debt, with an economic correction that will look like a collapse waiting if we don't change our system. It's also why we fight so many wars, because we're forced to cynically defend the oil backing of the dollar, lest we enable other countries to dump the billions of dollars they're forced to hold offshore as collateral. But if we want peace and prosperity, we have to change the way money works and that means going after the Fed.

In general, I think we should also look at more financial reforms to limit the role usurious interest can play in society.

I have never seen a society which makes wealth by taking advantage of the poor and desperate as desirable, and there was a time in Western Civilization when people would have rightly denounced such practices. We can have capital available without milking our people, and this is a conversation where I believe there would be broad consensus on all sides to empower the people by going after our common controllers.

Such actions will have cost and will cause economic disruption. But they will allow us to regain sovereign control of our future by our government, weaken international institutions that have a disproportional, corrupting, and elitist influence, and move the world toward a more peaceful and sustainable basis. People are not meant to have such power as these banks enjoy, and to have such command over an entity as huge and incomprehensible as the American economy gathered in just a few hands is the very heart of the corruption that pushes us into worshiping money over celebrating one another, and the battle we must win if our government is to ever regain independence from the banking cartels.

What follows will be complicated, but I think we need to rethink the American dollar. I'm not sure if the answer is to have specie backed currency which has value in gold or silver, or perhaps link currency to energy production as a more accurate entity, but our current petrodollar is both unsustainable and might be very well retarding the advancement of energy technology. To explain what that means as simply as possible, the US dollar once had a value in gold or silver whereby it could be exchanged for those tangible goods of value. After World War II, it became the world reserve currency, so sovereign nations would buy dollars and trade them for their value in metal which was depleting the physical wealth of the United States, causing the value of our dollar to plummet. To prevent this from continuing, Nixon put the dollar on a strictly fiat basis which accelerated the inflation and caused the dollar shock. To make the dollar worth something again, a deal was cut with the Arab nations in OPEC whereby American military forces would essentially subcontract to be their bodyguards, and in exchange, oil would only be sold in dollars, forcing other nations to buy dollars to buy the oil their economies require to function.

You can't understand American foreign policy until you realize our government constantly interacts in foreign affairs to keep the price of the dollar at a certain level and to confront any country that threatens to break this dollar driven cartel. That's what many of our interventions have truly been about, including our newly revived interest in Venezuela which has started trying to buy their way out of their self-inflicted crisis by selling oil directly to the Chinese. When that happens, war often follows, because our government unbeknownst to most of our people engages to protect the value of the dollar, using made up causes to sell the public on the action.

If you want peace, the petrodollar must end, and in currency reform, the deal to be made is probably for American forces to begin withdrawing from the many places we inhabit in the world to a more sustainable defensive posture and to broker a cancellation of many of our sovereign debts in exchange for this drawdown. We would find the world a more hospitable place, have more assets to assist us with our own domestic development, and have true choice over our future instead of being subject to an international banking mafia of which the Federal Reserve is but one part. It takes vision, courage, and being willing to overcome the likelihood America will be painted as a pariah by the media who has long been in bed with finance through certain familiar and institutional connections. But using our forces for self-defense only, as most Americans have long since wanted, means we could uniquely shift the world away from bank control and back to the people within not just our nation, but many others who also wish to be free.

It's a good dream and one that better leadership could enact. End the Fed and liberate America. Because we don't want the sort of wealth that only takes and doesn't build, and because our government has been owned by these people for far too long. Both parties are guilty here, and it will take a new crop of leaders from all sides to make this happen.

We can't keep indefinitely robbing the future to pay for today, which is what we basically do when we keep putting off interest and inflation and asking our people to work harder to earn less so we don't have to abandon this broken system. We can talk about it at the bigger level as with the Fed, but the same bankrupt mentality also underlies our education system, which is why many of the same lessons will apply to the colleges and universities.

Education and Indoctrination

In a healthier nation, education would be used to integrate people together in unity and with respect for our nation, culture, and traditions, but the foxes have taken over the proverbial hen house. Instead of having our schools encourage our children to love America and our history, the people who like America least overwhelmingly dominate education and we've let them instruct at least several generations of our youth and young adults into thinking America is a terrible place. While I think there is always room for reconsideration and dissent, the reality is we have a hostile foreign culture occupying our schools and part of what we need to do is remove them.

Harsh language, but the logic is sound if you care about national unity. We need our children to grow up with a common language, common set of values, a love of excellence, and to encourage continuity between generations by rejecting this egalitarian practice of turning every generation as well as every group against one another. What makes this even harder to accomplish is most people on the Right who are aware of these problems do not believe the proper venue to address this is at the national level, even as the Left has been pushing standards where possible at every level, including not just the state, but the colleges, publishing industry, and their involvement in high finance. Given the extent of their dominance and the urgency of the crisis, I begin to believe we should look at national involvement in several ways.

First, I think we should mandate a national civics curriculum that encourages love for the country, a basic understanding of how our government functions, and we should require American citizens to be able to at least pass the same tests immigrants have passed to earn their status in order to vote. It's ridiculous to me that we have people voting who know nothing about government, are functionally illiterate, and who are not being taught by our public education to even understand things so simple as knowing the three branches of government. Such education should be mandatory, be in English as the common language of discourse, and should continue throughout the primary process.

We should also do periodic reviews of what is being taught in the most commonly applied textbooks to ensure high quality standards and to rebuke the common core curriculum. I recently had to read one of these textbooks for my niece, and the way they were teaching people was deliberately designed to take away the analytical tools needed for self-determination, and instead encourage estimation and conformity. The label re-branded the book to assuage parental concerns, but one thing good government can do is provide critical and unbiased commentary upon what is made for public consumption, including our texts. We want to make sure these no longer degrade any Americans, our history, or our heritage, and that should be the common standard up through college education when more difficult ideas may be addressed with the nuance and consideration they deserve.

I know the Marxists dominate the universities and they use the tenure process to avoid accountability while also deliberately restricting voices whose views are right of center from being able to reach the students. I saw it even when I was back in college, and the safe space echo chamber that has been subsidized by the state must end. Now, freedom of speech and association compels us to admit these people have the right to be heard, but what we need no longer do is subsidize their lifestyles and these ridiculous costs for tuition with government backed student loans.

To that end, I propose the following. The US government will no longer back student loans. Furthermore, to ensure the financial well-being of the prospective students as well as those stuck in debt, we will reopen bankruptcy procedures for those who have student loan debt. While I believe in the value of education, our willingness to back loans without any collateral, and often for majors with an earning potential too low to pay back the loans required to achieve them, creates in many cases lifetime burdens that can never be discharged and have also artificially inflated the cost of higher education to the benefit of professors and financial aid offices at the direct cost of students and parents.

There will always be demand for high quality education, but the cost of college tuition has been insane for many years, and only when we stop subsidizing loans and allow the market to determine the quality and value of education will we see costs drop as well as a more realistic balance of ideas, courses of study, and institutional pathways. Free choice will liberate education from the grasp of those who essentially are funded by taxpayers to teach such vitriol, and it will benefit the students who will now no longer have to enter into decades of financial hardship just to go to school.

Another idea I have in a similar vein is to allow a one-time student rebate for accumulated loan debt. I have little sympathy for those who cynically made money off those students going to these colleges where so much of what is currently taught appears to have such little practical value. When a person buys a product that doesn't perform, they're permitted a refund in many cases, and such action seems sound to me here. Instead of watching a generation flounder for a decade to pay back debt, which is also a means by which compliance with the politically correct social order is maintained, we're going to liberate our people from debt where we can, and this is a good place to start.

How to best accomplish this is a conversation we should develop, but the goal is to empower students, free our people, and to bring the university into balance. I'm not against a fair market value for education, but that is not what we have, and we probably have too many colleges that teach propaganda and not nearly enough trade schools that teach skills which would have real financial value and improve the lives of our people. I would love to see a better balance between these two and think that changing how college financing works is a big step in the process.

Beyond this, I think it's worth looking at how we expand parental choice in education. There are major problems with having the state dictate the entire curriculum, and I'm incredibly sympathetic to those who choose to home school or send their kids to charter schools and other alternative means of education. It seems like the tax dollars to pay for the school should follow the child instead of the residence and moving away from the strictly geographic model to something more balanced and free-form would be healthy. Vouchers are one option to encourage school choice as would be tax rebates.

It's an area of particular concern to both rural residents and inner-city residents alike whose geographic constraints limit the social mobility of future generations. Being born in a place where the schools aren't up to par shouldn't constrain our children from having access to excellent education. I don't think the answer is to forcibly move people from their homes and into other districts, but rather to create incentives to bring the better education to where the people are, and we should think about how partnerships could be realized to achieve educational excellence.

This is one area where nonprofits could potentially be of assistance. I'm notorious for criticizing all the terrible social policies where we see corporations give money to support causes that only increase division and set us against one another. It's worth considering massive restructuring of where charitable contributions can be permitted, with a mind perhaps to redirecting corporate money away from social justice activism and instead toward pro-American educational support for schools in economically impoverished areas. Much of the money in their life cycle comes from government grants anyway, so it makes sense to have these indirect moneys go to where they can have greatest benefit.

Beyond what we can mandate, one thing I will do constantly is use the power of the bully pulpit to speak to what quality education looks like. We need high standards, but not in the sense of teaching to the test, but to creating analytical minds encouraged to understand the world, see nature as it is, have a firm command of reason, and be engaged in the world. For too long, we've had a process where certain preordained conclusions are simply pushed and reaffirmed with all countervailing viewpoints dismissed, removed, or punished. As someone who comes from the heterodox school, I will push for the challenges to be fairly examined, and to let the facts determine the case of what happens without the false dogmas we see come from the university.

Safe spaces will be gone. People will not be fired for being politically incorrect. We will find the truth, and once again we will value truth above tact and sensitivity. Quite frankly, we've wasted too much time on this idea that feelings trump reality, and I will attack that with a sledgehammer at each and every opportunity, because a society based upon such fantasy for ideology will self-destruct. If that is a little tough, then I think that a good thing because we need to toughen up as a country and have standards.

For teachers, I want to say thank you for doing a difficult and often thankless job. We want parents to be part of the process, but to back you and your authority as you hold our children to standards once more. The push for social promotion and the idea that everyone must automatically succeed is an abomination if it comes without the actual progress that excellence demands. We want to give you tools to teach creatively, to teach honestly, and to not force you to aim for the lowest common standard. I accept that for us to reach the highest standards, not everyone will always make it, and will support this push toward incentivizing our best and brightest while we also act realistically and find opportunities for people whose skill sets are not necessarily academic to contribute and have a high quality life.

There's a lot we have to do to fix education, but what we cannot do is simply say it is not the government's problem, because that is isn't working. I reject, as ever, the idea that just because government might screw up, that we are better served waiting for the people who will surely misuse this authority to overstep bounds we perceive that they will not follow. While I agree it would have potentially been better had a different system been created from the outset, we have to work within the bounds of what our children experience, and we simply do not have the time to claim we are above fixing these issues as best we can until better solutions result with better people.

The demographic research which is the heart of my argument shows that our schools are where our children are most commonly turned against this country and toward a future that only leads toward pain, conflict, and disappointment. Just as with the media, where I argued we need to support independent voices and local control, but within a national framework of unity, the same basic principle applies here in education and everywhere the socialist Marxist rot has corrupted. We need to take back our future by reaching our youth, and it is a project that will be to the benefit of all Americans and will require far more vision than finances, because the real cost here isn't money, but rather time and greater consideration from the parents and a better understanding of just what our children are learning to see that it comports with values we support.

While we can and will do what we can to improve education, there is no substitute for parental involvement in the child's life. You have to reach your children, and we will provide tools and support for parents who need help there also. Whether it is making more time for families when they need it, or offering some assistance to educate those of us who don't understand the new world so easily, I believe so strongly in investing in family life and I want you to be empowered to make decisions for yourselves so we don't have to have the state make choices for you. These are your kids and we can never care as much or do as well as a loving parent, and that's the core of what we are doing.

We want to give your kids back to you, so you can pick their pathway forward as they move toward independence. I know our society has done much at so many levels to take that away from you, and I will work to try to lessen those influences and ensure your voice is the loudest in your child's life, if you only make the effort on your end. I think that will make for a better America, and frankly, a much freer country as well because you're going to make better decisions than the state based out of love and hope.

Energy, Economy, and Environment

Given the proposals you see emerging from the socialist and globalist Left connecting these issues, I thought it important to offer a sane counter vision. You don't need to fear my development of a future where the combustion engine is banned and we all have to travel on bicycles and solar power. The extent to which they've allowed their obsession with climate change, another belief that far transcends the problematic evidence which has been accumulated in its support, is truly frightening. But I've often thought the reason they are encouraged to fixate on that problem is because it encourages global organization, which they love as universalists. It takes power away from the people to make choices for themselves and gives it to large and unaccountable institutions.

This campaign, at its heart, is about returning power to the people and to the most local level possible, so what I will not propose are any far-reaching environmental regulations, nor will I seek to constrain the economic boom happening here in the United States in energy development. I believe independence and autonomy serve us well, and that we have become a net energy producer means no longer having to be so reliant upon fuel sources from areas of the world which have been nothing but trouble for us. It also has created a large number of manufacturing jobs that help sustain American families, and every business and consumer benefits from having access to cheaper energy.

That said, I do recognize the inherent nature of these fuel sources is limited, and support investment into renewable fuel sources for the future. It would be ideal if we could discover a better energy source and find solar, wind, geothermal, or hydro power to supplement and replace other sources to drive down costs, meet consumer demand, and allow a diversified energy matrix. One thing I've long thought is we don't utilize hydro power nearly enough, given that it is a proven and relatively environmentally friendly technology. So between tidal farms and new dam construction, there are many opportunities for new construction worth considering where it makes sense for the local energy network.

Another area related to not just energy, but to our national logistics in general, is our crumbling infrastructure. For decades, the government has spoken about the need to upgrade our energy grid, our plumbing and sewage systems, a number of the major roads, and the train network. Instead of spending billions for engagement in foreign countries to rebuild them as we have for many years, I would prefer we spent that money upgrading the infrastructure here at home. It is both an economic issue and one of national security as we are vulnerable to asymmetrical assault against our failing civic infrastructure, and we should continue the process which has begun to streamline development, reduce regulations, and encourage states and municipalities to undertake their own repairs and upgrades.

I think there's a happy compromise to be realized in this area by utilizing proven technologies to sustain our economy while we seek out new options that should hopefully have greater long-term sustainability. While the government doesn't have an interest in funding projects like Solyndra that serve only as money pits, a better method might be to encourage prize money and micro-grants to encourage entrepreneurs to offer private models of what works elsewhere. Ironically, we might also be able to do what happens to America in so many other areas, which is to use foreign investment in these technologies from Europe and Asia to import the benefits of their innovations for domestic use.

In the longer term, I'd love to see us move toward decentralized energy production and distribution systems as well as decentralized manufacturing with logistics that allow people in rural areas to enjoy the benefits of technology while they choose to maintain their traditional living environment and cultural situation. While many people love the amenities and convenience of the city, there are many others who prefer to live outside that bustle where they can raise families and live in greater safety in communities of their choosing. Both options need to be viable, and an area of unique focus will be in helping the country folk be able to sustain their lifestyles instead of the push we've seen for many years to force people into the city or suburbs.

Fundamentally, I think people are happier when they have space to breathe, and much of our political conflict is driven by this insane desire to sculpt one size fits all solutions and force conformity on one another. Decentralizing the economy from the few major hubs to smaller regional hubs is a worthwhile goal that will generate economic development nationally, and will begin shifting America back toward a lifestyle that was historically less combative. We have always been a country of open spaces and living off the land, and while things will inherently be somewhat different, it's a vision I want to encourage more to consider.

We always hear about this one vision of America which is cosmopolitan, urban, city driven, and diverse, but it's not the only path. There is a different one where we balance the city and country, where we can live nearer to the land, more simply, and with whom we choose to associate for better or worse. For years, I've watched this push to make everywhere just like everywhere else, seeing the government pay to import and move people from cities to the country, causing resentment on both sides as people are being forced into places they would not prefer to be. It's time for that to end, and the days of nonprofits seeding refugees into rural communities over the wishes of the people will come to an end. We need to realize that we can only co-exist when we live and let live, honor regional differences, and recognize that city solutions shouldn't be imposed on the country any more than the alternative. There are millions of Americans in this country, especially who live in small towns, who can't even survive because they're stuck in states where one big city votes for solutions which may or may not make sense, and then impose them against others. It's a problem, and one we're going to talk about frequently.

One example from where I live in Maine comes to mind. It's easy to pass legislation banning logging to theoretically preserve forests, and everyone up here is rightly proud of our trees in the Great North Woods. But what people who don't live in the country fail to recognize is those majestic forests exist as beautifully as they do precisely because people work them, harvesting maple for syrup and lumber alike, replanting on specific schedules, and making both a living and providing a renewable resource because of private development and responsible stewardship. So often, regulation in environmental areas seems to start with a good motive of protection, but fails to understand or care for the underlying economics of the resource itself or the people affected, and therefore simply bans activity with the rationale that people don't need to live where the tourists like to just play. It's a major problem that I've seen through Appalachia and the Plains and we're going to work to constrain this overreach where possible.

Now, with regard to the larger economy, I want to encourage innovation and small business development. One area where nationalism works well is as we want to protect and defend our intellectual property, and we will continue advancing these trade fights against seeing our products just replicated as knock offs abroad. We're going to work harder to defend our ideas and patents. We're also going to keep a close eye upon monopolies which form to constrain our economic development and be unafraid to advocate in both the distribution of information and goods and services, that equal access on the basis of freedom of speech continues.

I am personally concerned about how Google fixes search results. I know they've done it to me in the past with sites I run, and know many other people right of center who have been defeatured, and for a primary source of information to be so rigged suggests we might need to eventually see them or an alternative arise or undergo aggressive public regulation to ensure content neutral listings are provided. I would very much prefer not to see government have to jump into these areas, but this so-called "community policing" is just the latest Marxist doublespeak for censorship, and it should not be permitted. They should also be ashamed of just how they're engaging with China and other countries where they serve as the willing and eager censor of free speech advocates there to earn government support. An American company should know better, and consider this a warning that we're going to look at our companies who violate our standards abroad and hold them to account here in this, their largest home market.

I'm also worried about how Amazon is essentially destroying so many brick and mortar businesses. At one time, they had a free-speech model worthy of respect and of

America, unfortunately they have now started to censor hundreds of books. But even if this were not the case, having a system where one business runs everything is going to be a major problem. It's something we need to talk about very closely, and given the links between Bezos, the NSA, the CIA, the Washington Post, and so many bad actors, it is a source of major concern that so much power is being concentrated in the hands of one oligarch. Call me a cynic, but I worry when we create new Rockefellers because of how they tend to use their wealth to remake the economy and society how they envision, and the government has a regulatory role to play to prevent predatory behaviors and ensure new competitors can enter markets.

We should continue efforts to ensure that the Internet operates according to American ideas of free speech and free exchange, and this battle doesn't get talked about nearly enough, but it is a struggle we're frankly losing. As the world wide web enters new countries, we see an increasing push to regulate, constrain, and limit that which makes the Internet great. I see how the Europeans want to ban memes because they're upset that their people, whose votes they seem to so willfully ignore, want to speak out against the repression from their own governments. I believe in such freedom as an absolute value, and it is the very best of what America has to offer. For this reason, I support making America the free speech bastion for the world as our unique contribution to human liberty and freedom.

To that end, I propose making all information and digital activity which is legal within our borders applicable internationally as a safe harbor. We will not hand over information about the activists who use free speech to advance the cause of human freedom and liberty, and we will provide the open forum the world wants and has come to love. We will prohibit the use of any future social credit score where conformity is forced upon people through fear of economic or social consequence, and we will ensure the free political speech which we have always cherished is forever protected within our borders, and where we will allow our digital space to be open to people throughout the world who wish to be free.

While I believe as a nationalist that countries inherently have the right to choose what path they want to walk moving forward, an even more core belief of mine is that freedom of thought, of speech, and association is necessary for people to make those choices. Today we stand at the precipice of a potential age of all-encompassing surveillance and totalitarianism, and we must act now to protect both our privacy and liberty by recognizing that free flow of information, both good and bad, is an absolute right. Without it, not only will America become less, but the liberation of the world from many forms of despotism will be quashed and the impulse toward freedom will be met with only negative consequence.

The world is likely a safer and more secure place when the people of different nations can interact in forums where they freely exchange goods, ideas, and services. When we get to know one another, we find commonalities that defuse conflict, and the differences that are interesting and work within our distinctive polities. It's not a one-size-fits-all solution, but instead a realistic way to ensure a peaceful world that is connected not just by arms and the imposition of force, but a real economic motor for this new century that is also ethical and beneficial to most.

I know technology creates problems also, and we can talk about that. We need to be able to get out in the environment and not invest so much energy in the virtual to the neglect of what is real. But the Internet and social media are just tools, and while we must always ask how these things will work to our benefit, it's absurd to think mankind is even capable of avoiding our inquisitive nature. So, we have to embrace the future even from the Right, but we can do so in a way that is authentic to our traditional values and uniquely American in that we place no limits on these new frontiers.

Trying to predict the economy of tomorrow is a fool's errand, but so long as we prevent any one person, company, or force including the government itself from dominating, I have faith the innovation and industry of the American mind and the American worker will prove more than equal to the challenge. The government should largely stand out of the way, provide support when necessary, but avoid serving as an impediment as often as possible. We need to make sure there are opportunities for everyone who lives here, and the last point I want to make, is that we invest in our people instead of continually bringing in outsiders to replace us.

I'm sick of seeing these H1B visas exploited whereby companies bring in cheap labor from elsewhere to replace American jobs in technology and other lucrative areas. If need be, we will finance programs and internal efforts to train American citizens to do this work, but I reject the idea categorically that we need outsiders to make our economy work. Let's find a way to instead take the talent we have here and fit them to the needs of the businesses that exist, and stop this idea that it's better to outsource jobs or use foreign labor. Both are unacceptable, and we will work to encourage investment in America and Americans, and to keep a very close eye on those corporations who think they're going to simply access our market for their own exploitation. For too long, America let its jobs and factories simply disappear so that corporate margins could be driven up by using slave labor elsewhere to dump cheap goods on our people. President Trump was right to call that out, and that business model based on exploitation needs to die.

Frankly, we're better than that. What will drive the information economy of the future is the ethical consumer, so even as we transition away from how we used to do business, let's always remember people and their desires are the market, and in trying to satisfy these, we probably will create the best model possible. I look forward to the ideas ahead, and hope with optimism we can both embrace innovation and provide a better future for all our people.

Foreign Affairs

The government derives its authority from the consent of its people. I firmly believe Rousseau had the right of it on this issue, and therefore, I do not recognize unelected international institutions which lack that imprimatur as having any authority. My mandate will be to strictly and solely serve the interests of the citizens of the United States of America, according to the laws and practices of our land, and I will fulfill that duty without apology in the hope that we can exist in peace and amity with all nations.

Instead of accepting the bargain America made post World War II to serve as world policeman and guarantor of international commerce and finance, and the even worse agreement to serve as mercenaries for the Middle East states for both ideologically and financial reasons, I believe the time has come for America to resume our traditional foreign policy of peaceful engagement through trade and cultural exchange. But we need to remove ourselves from military over-extension as some would-be global hegemon. It doesn't serve our people and our brave service members, nor does it meet the desires of most of the world.

George Washington warned us against permanent entanglements and James Monroe asserted our security lies in the safety of the Western Hemisphere where the countries who are our neighbors could exist without foreign interference in their development. While the world is considerably more complicated and connected than it was back then, the basic principles of their thinking seem as valid as ever to me, so here's what I propose as a radical sea change in American foreign policy thinking.

We will begin a gradual drawback toward the natural area of our authority based both on common values, geography, and the logic of commerce. As such, the first thing we should do is remove our forces from the Middle East, Central Asia, and North Africa. After nearly two decades in Afghanistan, numerous interventions in Iraq, Yemen, Syria, Libya, and elsewhere, I cannot say that we have gained anything in exchange for all these expenditures that justifies the cost and radicalization they create. The triangular struggles between the Sunnis, Shi'a, and Zionists are centuries old, will likely never be solved, and are not problems we can or should try to solve. I wish them all well and peace, but it is not our job to ensure that peace, and I think most Americans understand our long engagement with Islam has done little good. Instead, we should leave them be, and keep them from coming over here just as Jefferson learned with the Barbary Pirates.

As relates to Europe, we should work to reform NATO away from this stupid contest with Russia and instead integrate them within a looser alliance that begins demilitarizing Europe against itself, and works with the Russians and all unaffiliated European nations to once again set up the Mediterranean as the sea border between Western Civilization and the Islamic world, and to stop the tide of human refugees pouring in from the Third World. It is the security issue of the time over there, and the European bureaucrats need to be told, as national movements in each of their respective countries are making clear, that their people do not want to be replaced by Muslims or Africans.

America will gladly help the Europeans to resettle these people back to their continents of origin, to provide naval support against the trafficking of any people, and make very clear to Turkey they are not to let people come in through the back door. This is a great opportunity to work in concert with Russia and to seek to jointly ensure the security, peace, and freedom of the European peoples within their respective nations to work for the betterment of their own people. As we accomplish this task, the American presence in Europe can be massively decreased, which is something Europeans have increasingly wanted since the end of the Cold War, and all outstanding issues with Russia regarding the borders with Ukraine can hopefully be peacefully resolved as new security cooperation can extend from the Atlantic to the Pacific, based not on a tripwire NATO organized against the East, but in common defense of civilization against the global South.

If Europe chooses not to participate in these actions, and instead continues their suicidal efforts to destroy their own populations, then America will not provide any more security support and will withdraw fully. My hope and belief is we will remain engaged with the United Kingdom, supporting its people who have chosen to dissociate from the European Project, and their island can serve as one of three toeholds in a new 21st Century Monroe Doctrine where America claims command of the Western Hemisphere in the name of free sovereignty for North and South America and all its nations, free access to the sea for all nations, and three points in our traditional allies of the United Kingdom, Japan, and in South Africa to ensure free trade flows smoothly, and that should the security situation change, we can adapt quickly.

The reality is that we face a revanchist Russia and a rising China, and I want to avoid the Thucydides Trap that will lead to another great war that humanity won't survive. For many centuries, power was maintained relatively peaceably in Europe through a concert of great powers, and we should return to that model by recognizing that Russia, China, India, and others have legitimate claims and aspirations in their respective spheres of influence. America cannot afford, nor do our people want to fight wars to guarantee the sovereignty of Crimea, Taiwan, or Kashmir. It's insane to even try, and instead, we should work toward allowing natural progression of great powers and to encourage this on a peaceful basis, recognizing our own such aspirations and limiting them to our core allies.

With respect to Asia, this means Japan remains under the American security umbrella, and I would like to see Japan also integrated into the security apparatus which replaces NATO as an informal understanding of the global and civilized North. Korea will continue its process toward demilitarization with a hope that the North and South of that country might eventually find their way toward peaceful normalization. I would like to work toward America leaving Korea, with the understanding China and America both recognize Korea as a free area, like Austria was during the Cold War. Peace is served by removing American troops from that dangerous area, and we should continue work to normalize relations with Kim Jong Un.

I'll be blunt in saying I don't blame him for seeking nuclear weapons. Considering how many governments the United States has toppled which didn't have those weapons, it was a sane decision for their government to make for their own survival, even as I disapprove of how they have cared for their people. Nonetheless, the best action against nuclear proliferation isn't threatening the use of force, but instead a sane international system where countries do not believe American or other forces will look to resolve conflict through military intervention, and we need to take the lead in renouncing this way of approaching conflicts where countries have not attacked us. I do expect in the short term we may see wars happen in certain areas, especially in the Middle East and Africa, but even those will probably see the establishment of more secure entities in their wake, and most importantly, they will not be our major concern.

With respect to China, they have a choice they need to make, which is whether they want to be an integrated nation within a new global framework, free to expand within their traditional sphere of influence, or if they want to be a

Communist pariah supporting globalism and the oppression of their people. China will be the Great Power of equal status to America this century, and my hope is to engage them in a serious conversation where we encourage them to move away from the corrupt ideology of their state and instead, as they have largely already done, serve the interests of the Chinese people. That government need not be democratic, but the corrupt Western ideology of Communism serves no one in the West or the East, and they will have the choice to become part of what I term the Global North of civilized countries or to be part of the languishing Third World. Just as Greece educated Rome, so too can America exist in amity with China.

In any world, but especially in one such as I imagine, the United Nations is pointless. I will argue for the United States to leave the UN, to no longer fund its absurd mandates, and to stop pretending a democracy of dictatorships has any value or sanction save as a debating society. In place of this organization, we should have an International Congress of some sort with the United States, China, and Russia as the three principal powers in its organization. I would expand this roster to include as affiliated countries leading for security Germany, Japan, the United Kingdom, India, Brazil, Australia, and South Africa, recognizing each continent with the major economic powers who exist within global civilizational norms. This Congress can serve as the basis to guarantee global peace through communication without all the useless pomp we see from other diplomats.

I also want to talk a little bit about South Africa as an area of specific concern. I recognize that Africa as a developing continent is an area being contested by many different competing interests including the Europeans, Chinese, and more than a few American companies. My basic thought is the global South will have to find its own path, but South Africa is a unique exception because of its Western roots and because it does serve as a foothold from which a better example can be shown for Africa. The increasing radicalization of that government concerns me, as does the plight of the Afrikaner farmers who live there and have been threatened.

Although I generally support refugees remaining where they are, in this one case, I would make a potential exception to see the White farmers there find refuge in western countries where their race would not be used against them, and whether in America, Australia, or Russia, to see them find homes where they can live in peace and prosperity, also allowing South Africa to then attempt to become a successful Black organized First World Country. I worry they're not on that path now with their radicalization, but intelligent engagement could shift them toward being the force that serves to stabilize and improve Africa from the south moving upward, which is a worthwhile goal. It's not a military one, but rather the recognition that the world cannot simply ignore a whole continent.

It won't have escaped the notice of many people that I've deliberately excluded the Islamic world from any global planning. That is no accident, and it's because I believe they aren't ready to be integrated in larger security issues because all I ever see is these people fighting one another and trying to spread their radicalism. Their newfound wealth and beautiful cities do not conceal the essentially barbaric foundations of how they interact with one another and govern themselves. It's no secret that I am not a fan of that religion, and until such time as they learn how not to hide violence beneath taqiyya, I think not just America, but the world itself does best to simply quarantine those areas and let them work out their own struggles between themselves.

Iran might be an awful state to its people, and it is terrible how the people are oppressed, but the root of why that was spawned was the stupid intervention of the British and then the Americans against a legitimately elected government in the Fifties and our cynical embrace of the Shah. We also funded Iraq for years to launch chemical warfare against these people before we decided that we didn't like them either. All of this lunacy has rightly made it impossible for America to engage there on a fair basis, and so I argue for disengagement. The Saudis will have to protect themselves and I have no doubts the Israelis are equally capable of doing so.

The national security establishment will probably be aghast to read that I suggest abandoning our defense arrangements with both the Gulf and Israel, but I believe the interests of all these states share nothing in common with those of the American people. Furthermore, so much American blood and treasure has already been sacrificed on their behalf without any benefit to us, that I think they should thank us heartily before we leave, and then work with one another. I suspect the Israelis and Saudis will continue working together as they long have without wanting to tell their people, and they can then figure out on what terms they want to relate to Iran and Turkey. War is hard and expensive, and absent using us as a free hammer, the Middle East might even become a more rational place which would be good for all humanity.

In terms of how I see security, I'm a pragmatist, realist, and nationalist. I don't believe in democracy as the perfect solution for every culture, and won't want to intervene to promote social idealism. America's job is to look out for America's interest, but out of respect for our many longstanding arrangements, the managed adjustment into a global security framework of many powers seems long overdue, and would represent a major savings for our country when we need to reduce our debt, fix our national infrastructure, and frankly conduct financial currency reforms to avoid collapsing our own economy from overreach. It's in the world's interest to see that happen, and everyone gets something in this plan with the parts of the world that are most successful and productive having the chance to work in common interest.

In our own backyard, I think we should work much more deeply to integrate our economy and immigration policy with Canada, seeing our countries as deeply and inextricably intertwined for both security and culture. We should also encourage Mexico to develop as a successful country and work with them to secure their southern border against immigration from states further south and to help remove the corrupting influence of drugs from their economy. We would be naïve if we thought our purchasing habits, and tendrils of our own Deep State aren't heavily involved therein, and cleaning up our mess at home will necessarily draw us into action down there. A successful Mexico can serve as it chooses as a home for the many people of that origin to become a better country, and as an additional bulwark against the global migration the United States will not accept and against which will we build walls and work for our defense.

We will maintain a strong and powerful military, capable of intervention as needed, and with the toeholds to quickly mobilize internationally. But we will move away from the mindset of intervention, and respect the sovereignty of all nations and demand the same for ourselves. Most American people support this policy as one of strength without aggression and principled leadership in concert with other powers. Removing all the tripwires and giving the world space to breathe as we draw back will save money, save lives, and replace a corrupt global bureaucracy with a far smaller and simpler edifice that ensures the important conversations happen while removing the idea of a single global government.

As a nationalist, I know what is right for us is not right for everyone else, and the days when America foolishly seeks to impose our values or our interests on everyone else must come to an end. We simply cannot afford this, and our people do not want to take care of the world. It's time we take care of our own.

Debt, Trade, and Taxes

I've deliberately shied away from big government programs and promises throughout this plan because I'm serious about one problem which no one on either side seems to even mention, which is our ever-growing debt. I sometimes think elites don't care because these people want to engineer a collapse as means to assume even greater government power over society, which is insane because if you realize poor state central planning is at the heart of what is causing this runaway debt spiral, why would you invest more power into the hands of the people who created the calamity in the first place?

Of course, they think that this will allow the creation of true socialism with mandated outcomes, and if they are allowed to spend as freely as they would choose, what would inevitably happen is a re-enactment of the old Soviet Union here in the United States. It's not something we want to experience here in America with rationing, mandated government policy, and political correctness ramped up to criminal offenses for speaking against our good and just government. The good news is we don't have to walk down that path, but it takes responsible leadership and properly managing changes.

Throughout this text, we've touched upon some of things we need to do to fix the larger problems ahead. We definitely need to change how the dollar works, moving away from the petrodollar and the Federal Reserve System, and to something new where we get out from being held as sovereign debt internationally. Frankly, there will likely be some inflation involved with the change, but if we couple this with the new restrained foreign policy that meets the international desires of both peace and many other actors, I think Americans might be pleasantly surprised about how much room we have to maneuver. As Teddy Roosevelt once wryly noted, a big stick has its uses and the current strength of our military gives us many options in the event that we consider a general default on what we owe to external creditors, a path we must keep open even as we can and should find better alternatives.

The other problem we have in our government is an insane amount of unfunded liabilities, which at this point nearly equal the entire value of the country. Our government has promised to pay for programs that we do not have enough revenue to necessarily support, and we'll need to think of ways to cover that gap. As people rely on programs like Medicare and Social Security for survival, we cannot simply cancel the obligations we owe our people nor should we rush to consider the question of how we should perpetually force people to live on less. Instead, I think we need to look for alternate sources of revenue to offset these expenditures as we always look for opportunities to realize cost savings.

Trump's emphasis on trade is relevant here. As a matter of national economic development, it's insane we have been fine with losing hundreds of billions of dollars in trade imbalances each year. I would continue his policy to work toward a zero-sum trade balance with all countries and to open up new markets to American goods. Furthermore, to protect the competitiveness of the American economy, when our manufacturers are forced to compete against international industries that are either state subsidized as they are in many places in Europe or Asia, or where barriers to entry are used to artificially prohibit American goods from being traded on fair value, we will not hesitate to use tariffs and barriers of our own in response.

I don't know how many people know this, but before the passage of the Sixteenth Amendment which permitted the collection of Federal Income Tax, our government was funded almost entirely by tariffs and excise taxes plus sending an annual bill to the States, apportioned by population. In that, there's a hint of how we might get ourselves out of debt, which is to use selective tariffs to protect areas where we want to encourage domestic industry as in key manufacturing sectors that are important for economic independence as well as our national security, and where the proceeds from foreign competition can help directly pay down our debt. A smart tariff structure could potentially provide tens of billions of dollars toward debt reduction, which coupled with restructuring of interest, might make this a problem we could beat within a decade.

Despite having the interest of a learned amateur on these questions, I'm not a finance or trade expert, but we can find people who understand the rudiments of how to make a balance sheet work and move towards zero. Frankly, it's something we should have done a long time ago with our budgets as well, and moving to a net neutral budget is something I will demand America adhere to unless we are in a state of war. It's a small thing, but it's clear that we need to get past these police actions and return to the Constitutional path of governance where a declaration of war is required, rather than undeclared and costly interventions.

Now, we're going to save a lot of money by drawing down our military forces and there are many billions more we can save in foreign aid. Because there are times when limited investments may make sense for our national security interest, I'm not going to say we will have no foreign aid, but I think we can reduce what we spend by at least half and probably three quarters without getting rid of anything essential. There are hundreds of billions of dollars we invest in foreign countries that could be better spent in getting America back in the black, and for programs we want to implement here. It's aggressive, but if we don't do this now, we're not going to be able to do much later.

This brings us to taxes which are the other part of the equation. As a general rule, I believe in low taxes and a simple structure. I always see Presidents share their tax plans which never survive Congress so I'm not going to waste your time by creating a massive policy which is really the job of the House to create. But I will emphasize tax policy that benefits families, helps and encourages American citizens to have, educate, and benefit children, that favors small business over large business, and works to close loopholes.

One thing I've observed for a very long time is how charitable contributions are exploited in cynical ways whereby large entities give money to either suspect causes or to friendly affiliated entities to avoid tax burdens by claiming zero profits. We're not going to allow that, and we're not going to allow all the clever means by which profits are sent offshore to beat the tax bill. A fair code where profits earned are taxed with a simple structure at an honest rate is best, but I refuse to believe Amazon who sells half of everything in America made zero profit. I will support those who look to fix these corporate loopholes, and if someone has to pay taxes, it will be these larger businesses.

It should be stated that corporations get the money that they use to pay taxes from consumers, so that corporate taxes serve as a pass-through to tax the purchases of people who are often already paying sales tax, and who are using income upon which they've already paid taxes to make the purchase. So, I am not favoring high taxes here, but rather that existing tax loopholes be closed. It is unconscionable that a hard-working family should fear April 15th, while a corporation such as Amazon with revenues exceeding $200 billion should pay no tax.

Under no circumstance will I support a 70% marginal rate like I see the crazies on the Left pushing to adopt. It's as if they developed a plan to deliberately destroy the American economy so that they can enact their sick fantasies upon us. As we've seen in many of our own states, what happens with such poor planning is capital flight and you end up with places where everyone is dependent upon welfare and all the people with money move somewhere else. I've seen that too much here in lower New England to pretend it is a good idea, and we need to be realistic in that if Americans are not allowed to keep most of what they earn, they will not try nearly so hard to make money.

I'm not against wealth because I think people deserve the benefit of their excellence. Especially for people who work hard as opposed to those who simply inherit their money, they have the right to enjoy their benefits, and as they do, that money flows back into the economy. I reject the simple argument of class and resentment that suggests people don't have the right to keep what they earn, and having been both a manager of a town and in a sizable industrial enterprise, I've seen that money in the hands of entrepreneurs flows far more quickly and deeply back into productive efforts.

That isn't to say I don't think there needs to be a bottom also, but the reality which people have a hard time accepting is that the way to create the most wealth is to place as few limits on the top levels of achievement as can be managed. I've spoken throughout this book about the times when there needs to be action to prevent monopolies or the accumulation of too much power, but for the most part, I want a wealthier America because that gives our people the freedom to enjoy our liberties and, invested wisely, serves to the greatest benefit of all our people.

Contrast that with the cultural Marxist message at the heart of the progressive Left. Their obsession with equality forces poverty as an end goal because should two different people both have opportunity and both make gains where each does better than they would in mandated system, these people call it unjust because the outcomes are unequal. They rage against how one person becomes four times as wealthy but another only doubly so, and they use such resentment and envy in all their constituent groups to make all the economic outcomes seem like a cruel trick.

It's something I talk about in other books where the Right trying to sell itself as responsible economic stewards never reaps any electoral reward for two reasons. First, when people fail they blame the government, but they gladly take credit for any success without noting the policies that underwrote their profit. Secondly, an economy which rewards excellence usually does increase disparity at the same time that wealth rises within the whole, and that perspectivism from below is why the Left, in their desire to knock everyone down to the same level, hates financial growth. This phenomenon is why I spent a whole chapter pleading for why we must choose excellence over equality if we are to have any chance at a better future, because it shifts the focus to production of content or ideas and away from the always unhappy questions of distribution.

It's also an optimistic philosophy. I think people can do better always, and we shouldn't be afraid to hold people to account. Yes, there are times one has to be harsh and strident, and there are fights that come from calling people out for things they do that are stupid, but that's better than retreating into a world driven by feelings where we see grown adults basically sucking their thumbs and crying that life isn't fair. Of course, it isn't. Nature never made that promise, but we do have the chance to achieve, to overcome, and to find value in the struggle and in what we make of ourselves.

The world isn't going to be fair to America either, so we need to look out for ourselves. We need to reduce our debt by whatever means necessary and the best terms we can take through our wits and strength. We need to run a balanced budget and work unapologetically for our national benefit. So often, people in our media complain about how we're not considering how other nations will benefit, and I ask: Why should we? It's not our job, and you can be very certain they look out for either their own interests, or in too many cases, the corrupt influences that control bureaucrats and leaders alike in foreign nations against the interests of their own people. Never trust anyone who isn't mindful of your individual, group, or national interest, and with what I advocate, I always bring those points forward as I look for limited but more intelligent taxation, balanced and fair trade, and using tariffs to help knock down our debt to a manageable level within sound budgeting.

The alternative is to pretend whatever we want to be true can be. That's the heart of not just Leftist but also global economics where they keep making things out of thin air. You can do that for a while, especially if others agree to play make believe with you, but when reality hits as it always must and the bottom falls out, you can't really complain either. Because if you build your government and economy on fantasy, which frankly we have done with our myths of actualized equality, of pretending people are all identical, and the funny money that pushes all around, then I'm not sure how the system can work. It can only endure through fear, deceit, and quite a bit of implied or actualized force, which is a sad commentary on what America has become.

We can and must do better than that or we won't survive. The clock is ticking on whether or not we want to reset to reality, but I've tried within the limits of my own reason and creative thinking to bridge a pathway back to the future. However, I can assure you if we don't find a path soon, you better be ready for a much harsher reset than anything I've suggested here. Because the one thing we do know about nature is it is a force that cannot be denied, and one ignores it at their own peril.

Family First

This book isn't just about policies, but is also about the big ideas needed to make society work. There is no government that can make policies that will help people succeed if those people live in contravention of nature, refuse to take responsibility, and treat morality as relative. Even the best designed government will turn to utter crap without people who behave well, and that's at the heart of nationalism. The people are what really matter, and so much of who we become is determined by the people around us and the environments in which we grow up. That's why we need a whole chapter to talk about the import of the family and putting that back at the center of American life.

There is no substitute for having a loving mother and father who are invested in raising their children to have a successful national future. While I understand there are non-traditional families who do the best they can, and do not intend offense to those who find themselves in less than perfect circumstances, history and research alike have demonstrated repeatedly that the best opportunity for success for the next generation always comes from having a mother and father working in mutual support, hopefully as a loving husband and wife, to teach values, give emotional support, and encourage development in the next generation of great Americans. Having children is an investment in the future, and one I hope more people will consider.

For too long, I have watched the media argue that it is ethical to not have children, to decrease consumption, and to instead give our society and our nation over to others who come with claims they state are greater than our own. These same people have divided men against women, mothers against fathers, and husbands against wives through both propaganda and a legal system which fails to recognize the valid rights of both parents. Such drivel has been absolute cancer to our society, and has increased anger, hatred, and loneliness. As a result of this destructive propaganda, entire generations gave up their chance to have a tangible stake in the future in exchange for the stuff of social status. I wonder how many people regret those decisions. Unfortunately, by the time many gain the clarity to question their past wisdom, repairing bad choices is no longer an option.

It's a personal issue for me, because my wife and I probably will not be able to have children directly due to health issues. So, I am no hypocrite, but instead saddened that Dana and I might not get to share what we've learned with young ones, and to invest all we've seen and learned in giving another generation the opportunity of life. It would mean everything to us to have that chance, and we may not. Yet, we watch others simply move forward without any care, thinking their children are just an obligation or seeing so many children suffer neglect. We see the selfishness of too many, who glibly abandon their responsibilities, and who only seem to care for themselves.

For all our wealth, it's an utter shame how we treat so many things in America as disposable, including the people closest to us. Maybe it's because we have so much opportunity and so much division, but I see how many families are broken apart and dearly wish for people to reconnect and to find healing. There will never be a greater love than between those with whom you share blood and kinship, and there is no experience more fundamental to both human satisfaction and any chance of national renewal than investing one's heart, energy and effort into a new generation.

In this chapter, I want to specifically address these thoughts to women, and to ask you to take leadership in telling us what we need to do to encourage you to bring men back into your lives. We need our mothers and wives back, and I ask you to think critically if these many years of feminism have made things better or just divided us against one another. Is it not possible we are two parts of a whole that are stronger together, different but both necessary, and our complementarity is the key to unlocking a happier society?

I've talked to so many women who have told me they were shamed against having children and against having families because having children would cause them to be perceived to be of lesser social value. Nothing could ever be further from the truth, as the unique and irreplaceable feminine gift is the power to create and nurture life, and in so doing, create a continuity between the past and future and just a speck of immortality. To sustain our nation and to benefit our people, we need the laughing and happy children to rise again, and we need parents who find the fulfillment no paycheck could bring in these acts.

Nationalists understand that a nation is its people. Our people are our future. Pretty much everyone else out there will tell you that the future will come from outsiders, who may be good people or not, but who are not our people. I'm telling you our future must come from you, the American citizen, and from a choice you make to take that irreducible essence that is you and invest that into the next generation. I want to create a government that will help encourage life, make sure people have time to have children, and that would go as far as we can manage to recognize motherhood and fatherhood as vocations in their own right, and to support and sustain these acts.

To be clear, we don't need babies just for their own benefit, although I acknowledge the infinite potential of every individual, but we need families that come together to answer the questions government cannot and should not. You are the inspiration, the opportunity, the innovation, the social welfare network, the education, and the answer to so many of the problems about which we stumble in our efforts to answer. Well-intended people get deluded into thinking the state can and should be surrogate for what loving parents naturally provide so much better than we can even attempt, and I'm going to push back hard against that by working to rebuild the traditional family for all Americans.

As part of this, I believe to my core that marriage is a relationship and a lifetime commitment before God between one man and one woman. While I respect that other people choose to celebrate love in other ways, I say without hostility that such relationships lack this unique capacity to create, sustain, and nurture life, and while government does not exist to oppress those who diverge from what is ideal, it is our highest social responsibility to protect and enrich life. Through elevating and defending traditional marriage as a unique, natural, and necessary foundation of our society, our government will work to build stronger families.

As mentioned earlier, I support tax benefits for children within the framework of marriage and two parent families, and will want to shift support toward sustaining these institutions instead of only sustaining the children themselves. The way to create the best people isn't just to provide for the material needs of children, but instead to try to bolster their emotional needs by sustaining the parents also. Now, there are clear limits to how much policy can do in this area, and I recognize this is more a cultural ideal but one which I will articulate often because of its very import.

It's a strange irony, as I can be a rather caustic commentator on how people relate to one another, speaking publicly and openly on the differences between groups of people, and as an outspoken critic of feminism. I know that is yet another of the -isms that is not supposed to be criticized, especially by a man like myself, but I don't believe it misogyny to suggest that women and men work together better as partners rather than competitors, and to suggest this forced social agenda that wants to feminize men and androgenize women is entirely artificial. Men and women are patently different, and while we certainly both deserve legal protection, equal rights, and mutual respect, what that means in practice to reach our optimal fulfillment might be quite different.

Call it fourth wave feminism if you like, but I want to throw out the challenge of discovering how we reconnect men and women in a way that honors the inherent nature of women and what you want. I refuse to believe most women want to live in this phony #MeToo world where every man is a potential predator, every father an oppressor, every husband a rapist, and every son a threat. As insane as that sounds, I see people on the far Left write such nonsense, and I know most women understand men are the same as they ever were, wanting to be strong, needing to be loved, and hoping to find a partner. I think we can reconnect on that basis, if women understand as they always have how to make their men feel needed, and to find the security so many women want in that embrace.

I know there isn't one vision that works for everyone, and as I make quite clear, individuals who diverge can find their own happiness. But for the mainstream of men and women alike, I think the happy path includes finding a wife or husband, having a family, and being part of a community where any success we have on the bigger things only serves as backdrop to loving relationships and investing our deepest energies into the future. I know so many people who already center their lives around that and just want politics to go away, and that's such a nice dream that I think we should take some steps in the direction of realizing it.

Maybe that's the quintessential human right we've lost: To love and to be loved. We give ourselves away, and trade sex like a cheap party favor, but we stopped respecting ourselves and expecting more. We've chosen for so long what is easy instead of what is good, and if I ask hard questions, it's because I think we've sacrificed our chance at something so much better. I know it isn't easy, and I won't pretend even the best wishes will make it work for everyone. But the future is going to be what we make of it, and I just don't think it gets better until and unless we put the family back at the center of our lives. It's how America was built and probably our best chance of a successful rebuild.

To make this happen, the war of the sexes must end with not just a draw, but a victory for both sides. It would be remiss if I didn't admit men have a role to play, to be far more responsible, and to step up and show leadership. Too often, it seems like men have shied away from masculine leadership and investment in our future by wandering into either fetishism or juvenile adventures. It's time to see our boys become men and to show the strength, courage, and compassion needed to bring women to our sides. No one would welcome this development more than women, but it's going to take improved communication from both sides, and we need to stop letting the media play us off one another. We are allies, not adversaries.

As for those who encourage division between our people, I will continue to be utterly ruthless in skewering their stupidity or malice, and their politically correct nonsense needs to shrivel into nothingness and the disrepute they deserve for being death dealers speaking against life and family. If I speak harshly, it's because I think of all the opportunity lost, and all those who grew up without love or care due to this cynical folly, and hope that many more are not lost. We deserved better, and this is yet another area where our elites failed us miserably. The good news is with a little sanity, we will start doing better – and quickly.

I know that it takes many resources to make that happen, which is why one area where I diverge from Republican orthodoxy as a Nationalist is with health care. To have happy people, we need healthy people, and while health care is an area where government performs notoriously poorly, I also recognize having no solution is not an acceptable alternative, especially to the people who have loved ones who are suffering.

Health and Wellness

I'm going to start this chapter with this unpopular assertion. One reason I think we have such issues with health care in America is that many of us tend to make poor health choices. While I understand many of these are driven by a lack of time, an overabundance of stress, and failure to find a healthy balance under pressures that don't recognize our humanity, part of any solution to the health care crisis in America needs to be better habits on our part. We need to eat healthier, exercise more, binge less, and make regular maintenance of our health through good lifestyle choices a bigger part of the picture.

It's a lesson of personal import because I'm someone who let my own health go for many years. I topped 250 pounds just two years ago, had abnormally high blood pressure, a short temper, and let stress get the better of me. There were reasons for why that happened, including having a job which did not agree with me, health struggles in our family, and the usual financial concerns with which we all cope. I won't pretend I didn't eat away my troubles consuming more candy and junk carbohydrates than could possibly be healthy, and I was fortunate to not face more problems than shortness of breath and hypertension. I share this because my goal isn't to regulate people into good behavior, but rather to encourage all Americans to make better choices.

I'm now well under 200 pounds and continuing my descent, and I can breathe easier and don't feel nearly so unwell. My wife and I are eating better, and as we've improved our diet, despite the fact we deal with her chronic Lyme Disease and the inflammation that recurs, we're feeling better than we have in many years. The difference is palpable, and despite having to deal with a condition which insurance does not cover, a terrible and deliberate oversight I swear to correct should this campaign succeed, even our own better choices have made our health situation more manageable.

Many families, however, don't have such good fortune, and I recognize that for those who are afflicted by permanent or acute conditions, having access to reliable health care is everything. Unless one has been victim of it, as my parents were, it's hard for some people to understand how a health condition can not only eat up all the wealth and savings of an entire family but destroy the career which paid for health maintenance. While the old model of having the health care provided by the employer used to work in an age of stable jobs and controlled medical costs, this system no longer works, and fails too many people. The employment-based system also serves as a major disincentive to hiring as the health-care costs falling on American business is an added cost that competitors in other countries don't face.

All this means we need a new way of thinking about health care. Single payer systems are increasingly popular politically, but they also mean rationed care, quotas for treatment, and the reality that hard choices will be made where people would not have access to premium care on demand. I don't think Americans will accept being told their condition is too difficult, too expensive, or their life not valuable enough to be able to get treatment, which is precisely where such a system will lead.

But we also know insurance has major problems which artificially increase the price of care by shifting the cost from the unhealthy to the healthy, and that people unequally use these services. No one wants to go back to the penalty that the Affirmative Care Act featured to solve this problem, where the poor were functionally punished for being unable to afford insurance and where the healthy were required to buy something they did not want or face a tax penalty. Such legislation should have never been permitted, and it's an unconscionable shame that the Chief Justice played politics in such an obvious abrogation of what is legally permissible. Nonetheless, it was one policy solution to a difficult problem which is: how can this country ensure a high standard of health care for all its citizens?

If there is one perfect solution, I don't know what it is and I'm not going to pretend to have that answer when such a complete answer eludes me. But I know some things we can do to reduce the cost and to improve the quality of care, and if we start with what is achievable, we can have better health care as we work toward trying to satisfy this demand. I also think it important to recognize, while this isn't something that is guaranteed to anyone, the public demand has become strong enough that anyone that doesn't have serious solutions for improving the public health will simply be ignored. I'm much more of a realist than a legalist, and it fits perfectly within nationalist thinking to invest in the health and welfare of our people to promote peak performance.

Let's start with the obvious by stating that our system is forced to subsidize tens of millions of freeloaders. We know there are many millions of illegals here in the United States who use emergency rooms and hospitals as taxpayer subsidized health care, and those bills do not simply disappear, but are passed along to the responsible citizens of this country who are stuck paying for the difference in the form of higher costs. It isn't said often enough, but the desire to care for everyone, including tens of millions of non-citizens, is costing us the ability to care for our own, and we need to protect our own people by removing all those who do not belong here. Furthermore, I would argue that save for those who pay for treatment of their own accord, America does not need to subsidize any legal immigrants with state welfare including Medicaid. Our ancestors did not receive special benefits when they came here, and it is entirely appropriate to restrict access to social services in all but the most emergency situations to citizens. I cannot say how many billions of dollars we would save, but I know that's a good start.

The next area we can address is prescription drugs. We should require companies in the United States to charge our people the same price they do to the lowest cost country in which they sell their products. It is only fair we get the same deal, and there are many instances where Americans regularly pay up to ten times the amount that is charged in Europe or Asia, so that our citizens pay extra to subsidize lower costs in other countries. Our health insurance system is forced to subsidize the major pharmaceutical companies, and we simply cannot afford such a system. I'm sympathetic to the drug manufacturers and the large costs needed to bring a drug to market, and we can look at more intelligent ways to limit liability and decrease regulation while still assuring safety and effectiveness to help here, but what we must not do is force America to pay the cost of drugs for the world.

If we can reduce the cost of regular health procedures, and maybe work to shift people who presently use emergency rooms in lieu of conventional health care by working to ensure all Americans have catastrophic health coverage through some form of private insurance, this better allocation of resources should also help encourage more responsible health choices, and conserve more acute resources for appropriate usage.

One complaint I've heard many times from medical professionals in the past few years is the coding systems set up under Obamacare made the administrative cost of medical service a nightmare, as was the case with medical malpractice and liability insurance. As much as lawyers won't like this, the reality is huge medical settlements are born by the entire medical system and passed along to other patients, and we should look at caps on liability to reduce insurance cost. We should also simplify and streamline all these regulations so the focus is back on patient driven care decided by doctors and with minimal bureaucratic oversight.

I know there is a shortage of doctors, nurses, and medical professionals, and it's something we need to address by changing the costs of entry into this system for Americans who want to serve in these roles. Our current model of importing doctors from foreign countries who come here to make more money after their home nations pay for their education has created a serious lack of people in this country who can meet these needs, especially with the cost of educating an MD in America being astronomical. Within the medical community, discussion needs to arise regarding how we can create more American doctors and nursing professionals.

Another major cost vector has become access to certain scanning and diagnostic technology on a recurring basis. These tests are now billed at many times the cost they were assessed at just a decade ago, and it's an area we need to understand more fully as we seek to return costs to more manageable levels. People I talk to in the field tell me there are many cases of corruption and graft artificially driving cost, as well as occasional shortages of certain key devices which we can work to remedy.

None of these is a magic bullet. But each of these actions can improve the quality of care while reducing cost as we have a national conversation about how far we should go to make sure access to care is affordable for every family. I very much agree with the idea we should protect our most vulnerable, recognize that pre-existing conditions require special help, and know certain people do inevitably consume most of the care here in the United States. As a humane country, we have to rise to face this challenge, and for people who fall into these special categories, learning how to control costs in these areas will be the key to our continuing ability to meet their needs.

Although it is an indirect way of dealing with these problems, another area in which the government can become more involved to help our people is to work to improve the quality of the food supply. Many of the additives used in our food are decidedly unhealthy with little nutritional value, and if our people were more aware the food they are eating is often downright toxic, I think they would make better choices and face fewer health problems as a result. To that end, one area where I would like to see more government involvement is providing high quality information about the relative nutritional value of different food sources, and to fund more research about what different dietary choices mean for our long-term health.

Not only do I support this with food, but I have a growing concern with all the various sources of electromagnetic radiation with which we are bombarded. There is growing evidence all this wireless technology may have a very detrimental influence on health, and we need more research to be publicly conducted to ensure we're not irradiated to major health risks. While some might call these fears mere paranoia, none should contest the value of research to validate or contest whatever claims are made. We need to understand what our environment is doing to us, and it's a question that I think often goes unasked because there are so many interests that would stand to suffer should we find out troubling data. Yet for our own health, we must be sure these technologies are safe.

I don't agree that the government should force you to act intelligently, but conversely, you shouldn't expect the government to protect you from your own stupidity should you act willfully and stupidly. In these areas, I'm surprisingly sympathetic to much research that has been done about the value of restraint and organic choices, but I still think you have the right to screw yourself up. We just can't afford to pay for everyone living that way, and so we need to solve the major excesses and ask people to care more about themselves.

With that, we should talk about drugs. I support taking a very hard line on those who are involved in creation and trafficking of hard drugs. By these, I mean cocaine, heroin, fentanyl, and the like. We need to put people in jail who sell these, and most importantly, put the people who fund the financial networks which internationally move these drugs behind bars. As with anything, when you get the money men, the problem goes away.

As for the people afflicted, I believe more in treatment and rehabilitation than incarceration. Putting addicts in jail only adds cost to an already overworked social welfare system, and we should reserve those spaces for people who have committed violent crimes or major corruption against society. I support programs to encourage reintegration, and to help communities which have been impacted through both public and faith-based programs. There are many good people working in this area, and we should continue to support their work.

Lastly, I think we might be able to fund these efforts through marijuana legalization. As someone who lives in a state where it is legal, and who has used it before legally, it's my experienced opinion that it is probably no worse than liquor and has real health benefits against inflammation, represents a viable alternative for pain management, and could be a source of revenue for states to use as they so choose to help address their drug and criminal enforcement costs. I do not propose having a Federal mandate, but I would choose to see this declassified as a Class I drug with states then free to act as they so choose regarding legalization and distribution.

I won't pretend that it is responsible for a person to be high all the time any more than a person should be drunk or stuff their face with candy until they get diabetes. Nonetheless, people have the right to their luxuries and leisure, and part of liberty is trusting our people to balance these privileges with their duties to the public. Part of ensuring that is upheld is keeping strong laws against operating under the influence on the books which most states rightly uphold.

My collection of thoughts doesn't solve all the medical issues, but they represent a beginning toward identifying key problems, helping our people achieve better wellness, reducing costs to the consumer, and ensuring that high quality care driven by the patient doctor relationship remains paramount. I'm open to and encourage more help as we try to make sure we work for greater public health, high quality care, and to reduce the drug epidemic that has robbed so many of our people of their potential.

The Unborn, Churches, and Firearms

In case anyone doubts I'm a Republican, I have very strong opinions on all these issues which I want to share here. For too long, we've been weak in defending these moral issues and if there is a constant theme in all my writing, it's that we should make clear distinctions between our beliefs and the beliefs of those who oppose us.

In no issue do I see such distinctions between our nationalist embrace of life and the socialist love of death than abortion. I believe human life begins at conception, that the highest duty of the government is to protect and preserve innocent life, and oppose all forms of abortion. It is especially vile and loathsome to see the effort now arising in many states to essentially legalize infanticide, and you can be assured I will support any legislation that limits abortion up to and including a Constitutional amendment and requiring any Supreme Court Justice in the future to be committed to overturning the abhorrent decision of Roe v. Wade.

Furthermore, unlike our current administration which talks a good game on the issue but has not delivered, I will not sign any budget that funds Planned Parenthood as the single biggest and most wicked purveyor of these terrible procedures in America. The funding they receive can go to other institutions that fund women's health, and I would even support helping create a brand-new health network committed to family and women's health before I see another penny go to those people. Having studied the issues and understanding how they literally now sell fetal parts; it is unconscionable to me that our government and the Republicans in particular have not acted against this.

Such a position may alienate some but I will not compromise on the desire to defend our most vulnerable lives. Abortion is not a form of birth control and save for the very rare situation when the mother's physical health and/or viability of the child are at risk, and then only with both physician and maternal consent, would I consider any situation of allowing this procedure.

Where I differ from the mainline conservatives on this question, however, is I will support making contraception readily available up to and including permanent sterilization procedures. There is no greater human tragedy than forcing a child upon a parent who does not want to have them, and it is not my goal to force any woman into having children against her will. I believe, for the sanctity of life, in having readily available contraceptives not as an endorsement of a promiscuous lifestyle, but rather instead to debunk the argument that one cannot be pro-life and also be pro-woman.

I do realize there are some sad situations due to criminal acts this will not cover, but I cannot in good conscience place the blame on an innocent actor, the unborn child, for the sins of the father. For those cases, there will be government support and the potential for adoption to help the unwilling mother. Or, should she choose to keep the child, then that is also an opportunity for a happier outcome, but one cannot say they believe in a culture of life and support dealing death.

Also, the idea that the alternative to being pro-life is "pro-choice" is ridiculous, so this is not language you will ever hear me use. People who study the psychological impact on women who have abortions will share many stories of hurt, betrayal, intense guilt, and a longing for what was lost. The media never shares these truths behind their propaganda and cult of death, but we need to share these and to help women reveal that taking life is not a choice, but a burden which they should never have to bear. So, America will move away from being pro-death, and will move to protect women, children, and families as national policy as the moral and just path forward.

Despite all the propaganda to the alternative, most Americans actually support this position and believe abortion is made far too readily available and is pushed without any understanding of, and perhaps without caring about the full mental toll on the mother, not to mention the irreparable harm to the child.

It is likely my Christian faith impacts my position here and I unapologetically speak to Christ as being my personal savior, to His Grace for our survival, and in defense of the millions of Christians in this country who do many good works and are often defamed. While we protect the freedom of assembly for all faiths in this country, I want Christians to know the days of their persecution and defamation will come to an end in this administration. For too long, we've seen our culture and our beliefs slandered, and you will find me to be a strong fighter for our message and our people.

The nature of the Presidency is to serve all Americans and I must honor those obligations. But as part of those, look for leadership which speaks to the importance of moral guidance, which supports and features faith-based solutions as viable alternatives, allows for Christian education, and stops forcing the imposition of other values upon you. I've already lost one job speaking out for the right of freedom of association or dissociation, and this absurdity where one is sued into acting against their conscience is not something I will support. No longer will we allow those who want to unmake all that is good to force us into conformity with their twisted beliefs and you will find me an active and faithful culture warrior in defense of a revival in our country.

It is not something that I feature here, but my wife and I both understand that which is best in us does not come from politics, but instead from the spiritual insight within and from the efforts of congregations that speak truth and wisdom. My path is not to proselytize but to instead help those voices who have been drowned out be able to be heard, and I hope you will listen because as I've said in many places, a moral renewal based on love and community is needed to fix this country. Good policy may help and it certainly won't be as devastating as the policies which have had years to silence the moral leadership of this nation, but that important work will hopefully shine and maybe even serve as a force for unity, even as we have to go through difficult and painful conversations and disputes as we face new challenges amidst deep division.

I pray it works and pray always for wisdom and insight. The things we must do, let alone the things I'm attempting, are so far beyond my aspirations or abilities, that I can only hope the Lord blesses with the ability to overcome my enemies and to overcome myself to serve His greater purpose in seeing America's restoration from our degradation and loss of self. I can but speak honestly what my mind sees and what my heart knows.

I also know that may not be enough and we may fall into darker times in the not too distant future. For this reason, just as our Founders wisely counseled, I unequivocally support the Second Amendment and the right to bear arms. That provision was deliberately inserted into our Constitution to ensure the people had the right to resist against tyranny of all forms, and given that we have people openly praising communism who also advocate for gun control, it has never been a more essential right to defend.

Should I be elected, I will remove the bump stock ban which President Trump foolishly enacted, but will go further as I think a failure we've had on the Right is we've been fighting for our gun rights as a strictly defensive measure. I would support legalizing more types of weapons, greater capacity cartridges, requiring reciprocal recognition of gun licenses, and passing legislation to prohibit municipalities and states from unduly limiting these rights within their jurisdictions. The places which are most dangerous in America often have the most oppressive gun laws, and as I believe Americans have the right to provide for their own security anywhere in America, I believe it entirely appropriate to act at the Federal level to expand gun rights nationally. I also support removing the Hughes Amendment to reinstate the ability of citizens to legally own a fully automatic weapon.

The arguments against guns are rooted strictly in fear and lack of understanding and should be vigorously contested. As most citizens realize, gun laws do not punish criminals who have already demonstrated their willingness to ignore the existing laws against murder, but instead make our people more vulnerable to these predators, and such poor logic should be contested. As to how far I would go, my understanding of the intent of the Second Amendment was for people to be able to sufficiently arm themselves to contest light infantry in battle, as our Founders did against the British, and which we sadly might one day have to do against some future iteration of our own government if things go the wrong way. Furthermore, the 14th Amendment clearly states: "No State shall make or enforce any law which shall abridge the privileges or immunities of citizens of the United States ..." Therefore, state and local laws which infringe the right of citizens to keep and bear arms will not be tolerated.

I admit that is likely harsh to hear, but one thing I promised from the very beginning was to be honest with all of you out there about the nature of the struggle ahead. I very much hope my worst fears aren't realized, but part of why I'm doing this now and putting so much out there, knowing how I will be defamed and slandered for doing so, is because the time we have to reconcile differences and move America onto more stable footing is running short. We imagine things can't go a terrible direction here only because they haven't yet, but the historian in me knows better.

Now, for the valid concerns about crime, allow me to say I fully support local law enforcement and will work to ensure they have access to the best equipment to protect the rights of our citizens. I wish I could say the same thing at the Federal level because I believe most of the rank and file people involved with the various agencies do good and difficult work, but I also know there are too many Deep State stooges in there who think they are the government rather than those whom the people elect. As we deal with those characters in the aforementioned reforms, we'll be sure to acknowledge, honor, and support the good men and women who put themselves on the line for us.

I want to close this chapter by letting people know I believe strongly in values and will work to make the National Republican Party one that meets the expectations of our people to provide moral leadership in a way the old bought Republican Party never would. I know how many were embarrassed to vote GOP for years and had to hold their nose while selecting and then listen to years of excuses why we could never see our policies enacted or our beliefs defended.

You might have observed I'm not big on apologies and making hard stands does not frighten me. While we can always communicate with our fellow countrymen and compromise on policy to a reasonable extent, to compromise one's principles is the worst form of deceit, and a halfway evil policy is no good at all. From now on, we're going to play by the same rules which have been used against us for years where they are going to have to come halfway to our position instead of the long interminable retreat. I think you're ready for someone to fight for you, and I am here to be your voice.

Conclusion

For ease of reading, I've included an overview of my policies at the very end as a quick reference for what I believe and what I will support. If you need the quick version of what this most revolutionary candidacy is about, I hope that helps and serves as a handy and quick reference.

But at the end, I want to thank you for having taken the time to read and consider my words, and to express my hope that you'll listen to more of what I have to say and consider whether this candidacy is the one you want to support. I've never let long odds keep me from doing what I believe to be right, and I'm only doing this now because I don't think current candidates are what America needs.

I ask that you forgive me any excesses and mistakes I will make, and remember I am just one guy picking what I already know is a ridiculous and challenging fight. If I fail in getting every detail particularly right, consider that an unfortunate inevitability of the scope of the challenge which frankly faces us all.

The Left has gone clinically insane to see who can best reinvent Bolshevism and they would seek to take away every liberty and spend every dollar in America to make unrealistic promises to somehow unmake reality. Their obsession with equality has literally turned the Democrats into a death cult, and no sane person whose views are right of Trotsky could vote for these people and feel confident the country could survive.

Do not delude yourself into thinking they are insincere. The trail of bodies runs nine figures deep internationally behind people sacrificed at the altar of the state to enact the Marxist vision of Utopia, and the progressives here in America have had sixty years to sharpen their desire to enact policies upon us which will harm everyone.

Nationalism is far humbler than this. We don't believe in perfect solutions, although we believe in our people – our citizens - and in seeking morality through faith, reason, and nature in balance and to be good stewards investing in a future rooted in meeting your needs. I am a proud defender of America, our traditions, and yes – our identity. I'm unapologetically pro-White, but I'm not sure how you could trust someone ashamed to defend himself, and frankly, if you're a Republican, odds are eleven in twelve you're White also, so maybe if we loved our people, we could better relate to those around us in their struggles and understand that we can't keep replacing who we are without losing ourselves.

I don't think that is a crazy understanding, but no other Republican would dare even breathe that we're losing our country to changing demographics, so I will be the one to say it. We may reach a few others through education and culture of different races, but frankly, those numbers are always going to be small when we're contesting people who will gladly promise the sun, stars, and moon away from the majority to those whose resentment and envy is perpetually stoked and made to be limitless. I hate that our country has come to this, and reserve my strongest vitriol for those who have knowingly pushed such division, sought to replace our people, and who still brand people callously even as they themselves are the source of our largest problems.

Judge a man by his enemies, and my willingness to fight these battles is the best testament I can give to my character. I'm neither angel nor saint and not afraid to fight as dirty as necessary to take back our nation from these corrupt actors, whether they be donors, academics, spooks, bureaucrats, or even those bought in Congress itself or those who look down upon us in their dark robes. It makes no difference, because we must fight for truth, and we simply haven't the time to excuse ourselves from this battle. Our children will not forgive us and we will not forgive ourselves for what we may lose.

Lastly, I have to share how disappointed I am in our President. If he defeats me, I will vote for him if only to prevent the even worse excesses of those who have radicalized the anti-America message, but we all expected more. He was chosen to lead a revolution against a corrupt system but turned into just another politician who gives a charming speech and makes good promises, but never seems to deliver. Instead, he always has someone else to blame, and looks for new struggles and new supporters as he forgets that people elected him to drain the swamp, rather than swim in it with his son-in-law leading the way. Hopefully, this challenge reawakens something inside him.

I think I can do better, and I certainly am far more honest about the level of the corruption, the scale of solutions required, and the root causes of our division. Such honesty might make me hated, especially amongst the Left, but we are not going to save our country by half measures, and we don't have another four years to wait on Trump because he's a good guy or makes us feel good. I'll never make you feel as good or happy as he will, but I'll also not back down from the fights we need to pick in order to make sure our future resembles our past more than some dystopic novel.

But this campaign is not just about me, and that's what is different. Poll after poll shows the American people know we need to kick all the bums out. I invite our Democrat friends who are sane to do the same and send the communists back to whatever basement they crawled out of, as we wholesale reset our Congress and re-frame this republic. We might not have all the answers yet, but we certainly know those who have failed us, and whose lies we need no longer stomach.

Now, I've shared pretty much all I have to say and all you need to know to decide. If you have questions or concerns, come find me somewhere along the way and ask. I've never been afraid to speak out, and despite what you've been told, I'm mostly a nice guy. I like communicating, helping people, and being decent and civil to all who extend the same courtesy to me. I answer questions authentically and if I occasionally piss people off, well that's probably something people need more often than politicians who just promise what you want to hear: That you can have everything, everyone can be happy and no one has to pay for it. None of that is true and I won't lie to you just to try to trick you into voting for me.

You now have a choice. What you do with that is up to you. I assure you that I'm already doing all I can to help, but if you want to do your part, take leadership in your own life, help this campaign, or start your own to help in the restoration of America.

Come visit the campaign at www.endthecon.com if you're ready to learn more or get involved. It's your country – what will you do with it?

Acknowledgments

I always put my thanks at the end because I know readers don't understand all the references, yet this undertaking involves so many people. Is it impolitic for me to thank all the people on the dissident right who have been so maligned by our media, but who have shown courage to ask difficult questions, and without whom I would never have found the strength and integrity to stand before you today?

I've talked to many people of ill repute, and the funny thing is some of these men and women are the most loving and patriotic types you'll ever meet. It's why you should never punch right and stop letting your enemies define what is and is not appropriate. An open mind to new solutions is the only way we save ourselves, and I'm not ashamed to have many friends in low places because they're real people.

I also want to offer heartfelt condolences to the innocent victims of political violence that is rising on all sides. I've spoken vigorously against that, and one reason I engage so heavily with the fringe is because people who are left alone, beyond hope, to their own devices do foolish things in their frustration. It's something to remember when you're told to shun your fellow citizens that just because they go quiet, it does not follow they go away. Let us pray for the safety for all our fellow countrymen.

But one person whom I must first recognize and thank who is most certainly of the highest quality and virtue is my patient and brave wife Dana. We didn't ask for this life and, on some level,, I know we would both prefer to just quietly remain ensconced here in the Maine wilderness, but her support, her faith, and her daily courage in her own battle against Lyme Disease have inspired me to make this world a better place. It is a sad reality of modern politics that she is attacked because of her relation to me, and for the work I do despite not deserving such slander, yet she has never once backed down or abandoned me in the many fights and struggles I've had since my dismissal. I love her dearly and cherish her always.

There are so many people close to me who are helping make this a reality. The men of Pendulum have been an excellent brain trust whose wisdom and intellect is truly staggering as we've frankly talked about the problems in America, and I know their counsel has helped me to confront so many issues. They will become the nucleus of what I hope is a growing brain trust to replace the idiots in our current establishment who show no loyalty to either our people or the ideals upon which this nation was founded.

I also want to thank my friends in Maine, in Boston, and indeed, throughout the United States who are helping to catalyze this effort into something real. I hope to prove equal to your expectations of me.

I want to thank you, the reader, for giving me a chance and hearing my own words. Love me or hate me, I can ask no more.

Lastly, I have to thank the Lord, for giving me faith to persevere and courage to walk straight into the Lion's Den. I know I'm picking a fight that I cannot possibly win, but I'm reminded what the Lord said in Mark 9:23, and believe this is the right struggle at this time. A man can do no more, and I can do no less.

God Bless you all and God Bless these United States. Let's save her if we can.

Key Ideas in Review

America is no longer served by the political leadership of either party or its elites in media, academia, or business. They have deliberately chosen to abandon the people in favor of a narrow class interest increasingly operated along global lines.

To contest them, we must launch a revolution that is nationalist, populist, traditionalist, and realist in nature. This campaign will begin that push back to move toward honoring our people above system ideologies, to explicitly meet our expressed needs, to honor our traditions as guidance in how to proceed, and whose solutions are grounded in realistic expectation about both numbers and nature.

The national obsession with equality has converted politics into an obsession with identity driven resentment and fights over redistribution. Equalizing outcomes can only lead to death, poverty, and despair, and must be countered with a renewed national commitment to excellence which fosters personal and group growth based upon achievement and mutual prosperity.

For failure to protect the people of this nation, to show greater loyalty to donors than voters, and for abdication on countless moral issues, the Republican Party should see all incumbents voted out of office and be replaced with a new

National Republican Party which inherits the infrastructure and fights for all patriotic American citizens.

This party will then contest the Socialist Democrat Party and restrain them from their efforts to demonize the majority, break the rule of law, import new people by the millions to game the democratic process, and to institute totalitarian rule through censorship, coercion, and intimidation. Importantly, the Democrats are now beholden to the promises they made to the radicalized minority and identity subgroups to take power by harassing and disenfranchising the majority of our money, status, and position.

To achieve these ends, we must embrace nationalism strongly and unapologetically as we take down all the institutions which are corrupted, and use this newly taken authority, granted by the people themselves against the existing government, to protect and strengthen the liberties guaranteed by the Bill of Rights and to use the authority to root out corruption in both the public and private sector. It is likely substantial government reform may be required as part of this process, to be determined by the people as needed.

Our campaign will be a national effort, driven through social media and sharing information between people rather than donor support or seeking media assistance. We encourage everyone to become involved, to find local candidates to run in Congress, and to support this Presidential effort as well.

Our promise is honesty, integrity, and to face the real issues, challenges, and corruption head on.

Given the division at the heart of this country, and the real demographic shifts that are spawning a rising socialist faction in America, this campaign suggests we end all legal and illegal immigration into the United States for an indefinite period.

A Southern border wall will be built with the military to defend the full length of the border. Illegals will be returned to their countries of origin, with Americans who hire or harbor these people being subject to legal penalties. We will attempt to humanely remove all who seek assistance in their return.

Furthermore, we will disallow any future immigration to America, undo the Hart-Celler Act which created the visa lottery and chain migration, review the status of all legal non-citizens, and work to repatriate refugees to their respective countries of origin.

To combat corruption, we will seek to unmake the Deep State to ensure sovereign authority solely resides in the government chosen by the people. The FBI, CIA, and other agencies will face a deep review with heavy cuts and possible dissolution to follow. Authority will be invested in the military as needed to ensure the continuity of national security.

Furthermore, we will declassify all information as relevant to reveal for the public the full extent of any and all corruption, acting to limit the role of money and especially foreign contributions in how our government and various other entities operate.

To successfully combat this, it will likely be necessary to replace Congress which is why part of the plan calls for the removal of as many incumbents as possible, to be replaced by citizens legislators who arise through this campaign on a trans-partisan basis.

We will directly contest cultural Marxism by regulating the media and schools to disallow censorship on a political basis, to break up corporate monopolies, and return media to local control while supporting independent and free journalists.

Additional protections will be added to major Internet providers to encourage content neutral information access, to ensure voices of dissent of all stripes are permitted and not targeted for political, economic, or social sanction for exercising free speech on platform.

To increase national unity, all policies which privilege one racial, ethnic, or identity group above another with special protections will be eliminated, including affirmative action and diversity quotas. Legal protections against harassment and discrimination will be extended to the majority.

The Federal Reserve shall be ended, and the power to print currency will be returned to the National Treasury. A complete audit will be done of all measures taken by the Fed.

The government will act to limit the scope of banks and the role usurious interest can play in the future to protect the integrity of our money as well as preventing predatory practices against the people.

Student loans will no longer be bankrolled by the Federal Government, will be eligible for bankruptcy, and a one-time rebate or refund will be enacted to allow our young people to escape this crippling debt. These measures will remove perverse incentives for this industry which made money off our young people with the help of the government.

The expectation is such action will massively reduce the long-term cost of higher education making these services more affordable to citizens at the same time they stop paying for educators whose ideas are not sought or useful in the larger market.

For local education, we want to encourage parental choice and work to couple the tax money paid for the student to whatever school the parent selects, encouraging excellence, accountability, and choice. Provision will also be made for home schooling that meets high standards.

We support pro-citizenship education as a requirement for graduation, and passage of a national citizenship test as prerequisite to vote, along with a nationally approved identification card that clearly identifies a person's citizenship status for eligibility.

Maintaining energy independence is a national security issue essential for our economic prosperity, and additional development will be encouraged into both traditional and renewable sources with the long-term goal of sustainability.

Failing public infrastructure will be targeted for reconstruction including but not limited to roads, rails, water and sewer pipes, power lines, and information networks.

The new economic model will be designed to balance rural interests with urban ones to decentralize economic hubs in a way that permit people choice in where they live, to encourage national benefits in areas traditionally under-served, and to allow families choices for whether they prefer to live in the city or the country.

America will withdraw from the entangling alliances in the Middle East and return all troops home. We will look to draw down our commitments elsewhere. We will disengage from the Islamic World and limit our connections to them.

A new Monroe Doctrine 2.0 that limits our sphere of influence to the Western Hemisphere, the oceans, and having touch points in the United Kingdom, Japan, and South Africa will be the goal as we work to create a new global system to replace the corrupt United Nations with a concert of great powers centered around China, Russia, and us.

We seek peace and prosperity through mutual trade and will work to reform NATO into an organization that protects the national integrity of European nations, hoping to work with Russia to make this organization the beginning of an effort to unite the global North in peace and prosperity, while constraining global migration northward.

We will work to improve integration with Canada and help stabilize Mexico as a good neighbor in order to help ensure border security as well as economic prosperity.

The reductions in spending as well as reduction in foreign commitments will allow us to seriously address the national debt, refinancing money owed to foreign sovereign actors, as well as removing obligations to the Federal Reserve.

Trade balances will be sought to rebalance to zero with the American government protecting key industry areas against unfair trade and using tariffs to help our domestic production with any proceeds going directly to debt reduction.

Balanced budgets shall be required save in times of war, which will require Congress to formally declare it in accordance with the Constitutional once more.

We will honor all financial commitments made to our seniors by protecting Social Security, Medicare, and other programs with an emphasis toward improved service and cost savings at the provider end.

The family will be renewed as the central focus of our social life and nation, with marriage between one man and one woman enshrined with special legal protections to help encourage new children and parental involvement in citizen families.

Various measures will be enacted in the health care system to control cost including limiting medical liability, requiring pharmaceutical companies to charge Americans the lowest charged drug cost, reductions of waste in coding and price gouging, supporting healthier practices in agriculture and environment, and always ensuring the coverage of pre-existing conditions.

Help will be made available for those suffering from the drug epidemic with a global effort to undo the financial backing of the drug trade as crucial. It is suggested money from marijuana legalization may be used by the states to help.

Abortion will be opposed vigorously with an effort to help mothers and babies find as much support as they need to avoid this process. The government will help provide contraception as needed to ensure not one more innocent life is lost.

The war against Christianity in this country will end.

Gun rights will be defended, expanded, and promoted vigorously with the Federal government acting to ensure local jurisdictions and states can no longer violate this essential liberty with undue restraint.

Most importantly, this campaign will fight for the liberty, success, and freedom of all American citizens, attacking all sources of corruption, and offering a different way forward than either a slow slide toward collapse or the socialist vision of some new deal which is really a scam. It will be contentious but necessary.

America's best days are ahead, but things are about to get interesting.

Made in the USA
Columbia, SC
16 March 2020